Erin,

Thank you SO much for wanting to read my book! I hope my story can be an encouragement to you in some way ♡

♡ Jackie G

be free

JACKIE GRONLUND

ISBN: 978-1-54390-742-1 (print)

ISBN: 978-1-54390-743-8 (ebook)

Forward

By Amy Pape

Vulnerability, authenticity…and so much Nut Butter…

I met Jackie G in September 2015 on a camping trip. My first impression of her was all of us sitting around the campfire and thinking that she was absolutely hilarious. Over the course of that camping trip and a trip to Yosemite a few months later, Jax quickly became one of my favorite humans.

Anyone who knows Jax knows that she asks the best questions. They come as a result of curiosity and a journey to find truth. As a result, even at the baby stages of our friendship we got into some pretty deep conversations about life and God. I remember sitting at the kitchen table in Yosemite about an hour into one of these conversations. I don't remember entirely the topic we were discussing, but I do remember that I had new revelations about who God was through the questions that Jackie was asking me. I've never had that before, and it was a powerful experience. Jackie – in her pursuit of knowing the truth about God had inadvertently taught me truth about God.

There is so much that can (and should) be said about Jackie G. She is one of the most honest, vulnerable and authentic humans

I know. She eats more nut butter than anyone I have ever met. She is strength embodied. She is a fighter – she doesn't give up. She should not be underestimated. Jax is brave, kind, passionate, forgiving, gracious, humble, talented, and honest. I have gotten to be friends with Jax through some really great and some really hard circumstances, and all I know how to say is that I have come away from each of those experiences respecting her even more than I originally did. Jax does life really well. She presses into pain in order to overcome it. She invites her friends into the process with her. She invites Jesus into the process with her, and she emerges a better human as a result.

You are holding in your hands the story of one of my favorite humans on the planet. This book encompasses all that is so powerful about Jackie G. It is honest, raw and real. It doesn't hide. It isn't setting out to have all the answers, instead it's inviting you into the journey. Jax is instead inviting you into her journey – the good and the hard. It is a journey filled with hope and strength (and so much nut butter). It is a journey that will encourage and challenge and empower you. My encouragement to you as you read this book is to embrace the process. Let this story speak to you and move you towards God and towards community. In reading this book, I truly believe that you will find answers. I believe that in the same way my friendship with Jackie G has led me into deep and powerful truths that you will find truth in these pages. This is not a textbook trying to give you a step-by- step process for life, but this is an invitation to authentic living. This is an invitation into vulnerability. This is an invitation into strength and hope. This is an invitation to be free.

– Amy Pape

Prologue

6/28/16

*"I keep telling people to write books but honestly I
just want to start writing a book myself."*

6/29/16

*"Something special happened yesterday. I met someone who
believed in me. Can you believe that? I've always pushed myself
aside with things like this, like these are the kind of things
that are for my sister, not me. This is the kind of thing that
happens to my friends or people I work for, not me. But why
not me? I never thought I could write a book. I always thought
that was for someone else to do, not me. But you told me you
believed in me. You told me to start believing in myself."*

This is, without a doubt, the most intimidating first sentence I've
ever written. Am I good enough to do this? What business do I have
attempting to accomplish something as ambitious as writing a book
in the first place? Well, if you're reading this, then I just want to say
thank you. Thank you for believing in me enough to pick up this
book and put life and purpose behind the words I've written.

To be truly honest here, I have no idea what I'm doing. I'm just a 21-year-old girl sitting in a coffee shop, ridiculously obsessed with any and all nut butters, who decided to stop listening to the doubting voices in her head and take a risk. The thing is, I've been going a decent portion of my life not feeling smart or significant. For the most part, I've always thought of myself as destined to be the "sidekick" or the popular girl's best friend, but nothing more. Some say it's because I have this thing called "little sister syndrome," others tell me I'm just straight up insecure. Either way, it's not a fun way to live. Safe? Yes. Worth it? No.

Sometimes I don't want to talk to people because I'm afraid I might come off as annoying or uninteresting. I'm scared that if I show people how I actually feel and who I really am, they'll leave. Often times I don't speak up in intellectual conversations for fear of sounding stupid, or having nothing to offer. There's times when I get painfully lonely so I try to stay extra busy doing meaningless tasks to avoid the silence that, most of the time, has the power to scream the truth that I'm just not ready to hear.

You know those moments when you can feel that your life is about to change? The kind where you can sense in the deepest corners of your spirit that something is about to happen that will create the beginning of a major shift in either who you are or where you're going? Earlier tonight, that *something special* happened to me. I felt an invitation on a journey where I get to stop listening to those lies about who I am; I get to stop hiding behind the fear of what people might think, and I get to use my voice. That's a scary thing to do, you know? Because I can't help but think; what if I fail? What if my story actually doesn't matter in the way I thought it would? What if nobody actually cares what I have to say? It's weird how comforting it can feel when we stay on the sidelines. It appears to be safe out there, but it's actually the most dangerous place you can be especially if you stay there too long. The sidelines are filled with people who prefer to watch because they're too afraid to act. They're filled with people in silence because they're too afraid to speak. They're filled with stories untold, and voices unheard. Well I'm done with that fear, and I'm done with the sidelines.

For the past two years, I've been keeping multiple journals of pretty much every event, thought, insecurity, fear, excitement, and feeling that I've had on a daily basis. That's a lot of journals, and yes, that's quite a lot of feelings. Ironically, I used to think feelings were a bad thing, so I must be major a disappointment to my past self regarding this situation because it turns out that I'm quite the feeler. They go from me getting intentionally blackout drunk on a regular basis, to moving across the country where I knew absolutely no one, simply because Jesus told me to. They go from being terrified out of my mind of people not loving me, to being genuinely proud to simply make my own decisions. They go from wanting to die, to wanting to live out every layer of life there is to live.

I want to share these stories with you. I want to break the silence created by fear, and join the brave souls out there in the world that use their voices to spread truth. If you're planning on reading this book, just know that it's going to get really honest and it's going to get really bold. At least, that's the plan anyway. I've wasted too much time being scared of emotions and vulnerability, so now feels like as good a time as any to put it all out on the table and see what happens.

Shame

"In your life- over and over again- Jesus will renew- restore- mend- heal- inspire you through the streams of mercy that will never cease. Your life is not going to be about perfection or game plans- but it will be a loving and powerful invitation for those around you to step into the same healing waters you have known and trusted."

– My friend Meg

I WANT TO TELL YOU THE STORY ABOUT THE DAY that my soul was set free. This was the day that I made the choice to stop hiding from my mistakes, and come to terms with what was true. It was the day that I decided I would get off my couch and come face to face with my deepest, darkest fears.

Matt Chandler says that to be 99% known is to be unknown. That's crazy, right? I'll put it this way, if someone comes up to you and says, "Hey we need to talk…" and your mind automatically jumps to that one thing you hope it's not about, are you really free? Well friends, that was me for a year and a half.

Ever since that first morning on the tour bus when I woke up and learned the gut wrenching meaning of shame and self hatred, my life turned into a secret that only I knew about. But it wasn't just the mistakes I was making that I was trying to hide from the rest of the world; it was who I feared I had become because of them. That's where the shame was being kept locked away. I was absolutely terrified that people would see what I had done and throw me away. My heart couldn't take that. There were fears, feelings, emotions, insecurities... a whole list of things that I couldn't ever let anyone know about. These are all things that throughout this book I hope to go into much more detail about, but for right now I just want to celebrate the day that my lies were put to rest and my soul was truly set free.

This was the day that I was going to finally tell the one person that I was so terrified of finding out the truth, the truth.

On January 4th, 2016 I wrote in my journal:

"I feel like I'm falling apart. I feel like my world is crumbling. Everything from the past is coming to the surface and I don't know how to control it anymore. I'm hurting people, I'm losing people, and it's not even over yet. Tomorrow I'm going to have the hardest conversation of my life. There's no way around it. I can't live in this fantasy land avoiding the truth anymore. I need to face my demons and come to terms with the choices that I've made. This is absolutely anything in the world but easy. I feel numb but I'm breaking at the same time. How did it get this bad?"

I genuinely thought my life was shredding to pieces the day I wrote that. I just couldn't take it anymore. I remember this like it was yesterday, sitting on my couch alone in my apartment. Normally I would drown out the pain with an episode of *Friends* and a bowl of cereal, but instead, I just sat there in cold silence. I had been crying for about a week straight at this point, so my eyes were puffy and I could barely see the pages in the journal I was writing on. In fact the smudges of ink from where my tears fell that day are still there, and still as real as they were when they were shed.

Nothing could stop me now. I had to do it. I got in my car, blasted "Oceans" by Hillsong in an attempt to escape my pain for a second, and headed straight to my sister's house. I didn't want to wait for another "tomorrow." I was done waiting. I was done avoiding.

There was not one piece of me that expected a good outcome from this. I planned on telling her the truth about what I had done, driving away, and never being able to speak to her again. I planned on her completely disowning me and never wanting anything to do with me ever again. I planned on losing my big sister.

Hear me out, though. It's not that I *wanted* to lose her. That's the last thing in the world that I wanted to happen. You see, my big sister had pretty much been my hero for the majority of my twenty-one years. Throughout my whole life all I wanted was relationship. All I wanted was to be loved and accepted and close with her. Her approval had always been what I thought I needed to be okay. For as long as I could remember, she was the first person I wanted to think I was great, to celebrate with me when I succeeded, to cry with me when I was hurt. She was who I thought I needed to be like. I chased her around at school when I was little, begging to be a part of her world, just dying to be in her circle and life in anyway possible. Looking at her face when I walked into her house felt like a dagger just flat out pierced my heart. Looking into her eyes made me want to crawl into a corner and never feel anything good about life ever again. I was scum. It's what I thought I deserved. So why did I get myself into this mess in the first place, you ask? That's a question that took me a long time to figure out myself.

One of the hardest parts about driving to tell my sister the truth that night was the timing. After years of craving a relationship with her for more reasons than I could count, it wasn't until a few months ago, at this point, that that bond was seeming like it was going to take place. For the first time, Alex and I were actually getting close, actually getting to know each other's hearts. It's not that we didn't want to share before, I think we just didn't know what exactly to share. We didn't know who we were, or at least I didn't. I felt like the more time I took waiting to tell her the truth, the more I was going to hurt both her and myself with my mistakes. I knew that the closer we became, the harder it was going to be. It was getting to the point where she would ask me to spend time together and, no matter how much I wanted to, I would force myself to tell her no because it just felt like one big lie. I can honestly say that I genuinely hated who I was, and I didn't want to expose her to that. I thought I was toxic. I wasn't just on my way to tell her the truth... I was on my way to tell her goodbye.

Crying so hard I could barely even see the road in front of me, all that went through my mind were memories from growing up. When my sister Alex and I were just kids, we used to put on plays in our basement together with our dad's camcorder. (This isn't meant to be a plug, but if you look up "The Selfish Queen" on YouTube you might have a reference for what I'm talking about). We would dance around in our pink nightgowns and sing songs from the Annie soundtrack on repeat. She would pick me up and throw me on the ground and I would just smile and hop back up so she could do it again. Then the memories of me getting beat up at softball practice came up. Alex picked me up that day and as soon as I told her what happened, she chased the girl that punched me around the field to get her back. By the way, if the girl who punched me is reading this, I totally forgive you. We're cool.

That was my big sister. That was my hero and I was on my way to break her heart with my shame story, and say goodbye.

I parked my car a few blocks away and pulled over to try to calm down before I went in. I cried, I prayed, I begged God for a way out. It was loud in my car. Not the noisy kind of loud from the music or my uncontrollable sobbing, but the kind of loud that filled my head with fear. Fear that was louder than God, and fear that was louder than love. I came to terms with the situation, accepted what I was about to do, and tried to prepare myself for my losses.

I took one step into her house, only to then take one look into her eyes, and break down all over again. I stood there hysterical, barely being able to enunciate my words of apologies and how much she was about to hate me, and all she could do was tell me that she loved me and hug me. I wouldn't let my heart accept that though because she still didn't know the truth. I spent the last year and a half not letting myself feel loved by her because my shame told me that I didn't deserve it.

I was just a mess. It took me probably an hour before I was able to get it out. I kept stalling by telling her how scared I was, or running into the other room to cry on her best friend's shoulder (who had no idea what was going on but was such a good sport about it, by the way). Finally, there they were. There were the words that I was so scared of. There were the words that I thought defined my very being, and claimed me as trash. There were the words that I was fully prepared to hide for the rest of my life.

~

Okay, let's back up here for a second. What was this mysterious story that I was hiding from my sister that was so terrifying to tell her, and was it really as big of a deal as I was making it seem? As far as the seriousness of this story goes, I'll leave that up to you to decide. However, by the convicting truths in my own heart, it honestly did feel like one of the worst things I could have ever had to carry on my shoulders. If anyone reading this book has ever kept a major secret about themselves for a decently long period of time, you might get what I'm talking about. No joke, there were multiple times in church where I would sit there in my chair, watching the hipster LA worship band jump around on stage in their long t-shirts and ripped up skinny jeans and forcing myself to hold back tears because I was so certain that I was going to hell. That fear overwhelmed me, not only in church, but in my own living room in my own apartment on a regular basis as well. I would sit there, feeling about as heavy as humanly possible, begging God to take the thoughts out of my mind. I wanted a do-over. I wanted my memory erased, or something, because the darkness that I felt was unbearable.

Though in a peculiar way, I find my fear in those moments part of a genuine proof that God exists. That's proof because, in the middle of my mess, my heart knew that there was still a God and that he still knew me. I'm not saying that my fears of going to hell were true, I'm saying that at a time in my life where it would have been really convenient for my mistakes not to matter and the idea of right and wrong to not be a thing, my heart still knew that God was there. However along with that, the anxieties of facing him with the truth of what I had chosen to do were there as well. What I'm trying to say is that, even though my shame was overwhelming and my theology was all messed up, I never doubted God was real. With how strong the convictions were in my heart, I don't think it would have been possible. In fact, now looking back at those church services or nights in my living room, I do see myself all upset and scared, but Jesus isn't mad at me. My fears of him being ashamed, looking down in disgust, just waiting to send me to hell, were actually the farthest thing in the world from the truth of who he is and how he felt about me in those dark moments when I hated myself. I would give anything to go back and tell myself the truth of how much Jesus loved me in those moments.

Anyway, we'll get to more of the good stuff later. Let's go back in time for a minute to two years prior where the story began so my life might make a little bit more sense.

***

Have you ever woken up one morning and instantly wished you hadn't? I'm talking laying there, eyes not even opened yet and all you can think about is how much you wished you didn't exist. I was in the middle of, from what it looked like on the outside, the coolest, most exciting year of my life. There I was, touring the country with a rock band, labeled VIP at TV show premiere parties, living life in LA, all that typical rockstar stuff. If anyone were to check out my Instagram they'd be insane not to think I was having the time of my life, and that's exactly how I wanted it to be. And, at times, even I was fooled that I was as well.

Honestly, I didn't care if on the inside there were times where I felt like I was dying. My main concern was making sure that everyone who saw my life wanted it. I created this reputation for myself that I now felt responsible to keep up with. Every time I went back home to Colorado, I felt pressure to have fancy stories to tell or else nobody would care that I was there. I felt like if I didn't present this image of having the most exciting life ever in LA, people wouldn't love me. If people didn't love me, what was I worth? But if someone were to ask me at the time, I never would have admitted it. Instead, I just continued to go to party after party and participate in meaningless conversation after meaningless conversation, never actually talking about what was really going on in my head. Life felt like one big game. The truth is, I let my whole identity rest on what other people thought of me. I'm sure my fellow recovering people-pleasers can agree, it's absolutely exhausting. I thought that unless I could impress people with cool stories, I would get forgotten about. So every time I went home, I was stuck in this cycle of having to one-up myself, and honestly, it might as well have been based on a lie.

So then, what was really going on with me that morning? If my life was as exciting as it looked on the outside, why didn't I want to be a part of it anymore? To put this in the most simple stripped down form, the answer is shame.

Brene Brown defines shame as, "the intensely painful feeling or experience of believing that we are flawed and therefore unworthy of love and belonging." The reason I woke up that morning on the tour bus and wanted to be dead was because the night before, I had done something that I thought made me pure garbage. What I'm about to tell you is something that, for over a year, I believed I was going to take to my death bed with me. I believed that partially because people had told me to do so, and partially because I genuinely thought that there was no other way out. This is something that I believed to be so despicable that if anyone were to find out, they would see me as the piece of trash I truly believed that I was and never speak to me again. That right there is called shame.

You see, my older sister was involved with this guy for about two years. This wasn't just a casual thing that ended. For my sister, this was an intensely damaging relationship that, at the time, I really didn't know anything about. This guy also happened to be my boss, source of income, sense of security, and supplier of the lifestyle that gave me my "cool kid" identity. In other words, my world pretty much revolved around him, which is just unhealthy in any context.

Two days prior to my morning of shame, my sister and this guy broke up. The night before my morning of shame, her ex-boyfriend, my boss, drunkenly made a move on me, and I didn't do a single thing to stop it. I made the choice that night to kiss my sister's ex-boyfriend. I didn't know it yet, but that night was the start of year and a half long cycle of secrets and mistakes that I would never be able to take back.

So there I was the next morning, laying in my bunk, wishing that I didn't exist. I stared at the ceiling, half hungover from the alcohol and half just emotionally sick. I couldn't think of a way out. I honestly wished I had some sort of disease or something to get me out. Nobody could ever find out about this. This was now the one thing that, from that day forward, I thought made me unlovable; the one thing that I couldn't undo, and now I deeply feared defined me. However, it didn't really matter how hard I tried to keep it a secret or not, because I still knew about it. As long as I knew what had happened, I considered myself unworthy of love and quickly learned to hate myself instead. If people showed me love I would be gracious on the outside, but on the inside my heart was saying, "yeah but you wouldn't love me if you only knew this about me." I was terrified, and the only person who I could talk through it with was the one who I had made the mistakes with in the first place. We kept coming to the conclusion that we should never tell anyone, and we couldn't let it happen again, but guess what happened the next night? The same thing. We ended up in this endless cycle of getting drunk, making out, and so on, then waking up smothered in shame, swearing to make that *the last time.*

The thing that I felt the most ashamed of the next morning was that I was the one who made the choice the night before to go out. I was the one who chose to drink the drinks with him, knowing very well what was most likely going to happen. There was a rebellion going on in my heart that made no sense. It was like I was so desperate to feel loved and cared about that I used this as a way to feel that. I knew it was wrong, but I wanted to keep doing it. Why did I want to be a part of something that I knew I hated so much?

What is it about shame that has such an overbearing authority over our lives, and why on earth do we give it the power to tell us who we are and what we deserve? It has this intoxicating way of making us feel as though we're hopelessly defective, so it keeps us silent and slowly eats away at our souls. What's really frustrating about shame in my opinion, is that it's all based on a lie. In a spiritual context, that lie is straight from the mouth of the enemy. It's something that's been around since day one in the garden. The moment the serpent told Eve to eat the forbidden fruit, she felt shame from her nakedness before God. In my opinion, Eve was covering up more than just her naked body in that moment. Think about it, she had been naked every other day of her life and never thought anything of it. If naked was all she knew, why was it *now* something to be ashamed of? Why was it *now* something that needed to be covered up? I believe that Eve was covering herself up physically because the shame from what she had just done made her believe that she was messed up. It wasn't guilt speaking saying she made a mistake; it was shame saying that she *was* a mistake. What happened next in the garden makes perfect sense now, thinking of it in that context. After her shame convinced her to cover up on the outside, she hid. She covered herself and hid, just like we do today. Like Eve, when I felt shame from my mistake I also covered myself up on the outside by putting on a big smile and making every effort I could to prove to people that I was okay. I overcompensated with fancy Instagram posts and even more exciting stories. If any of my friends were to hear how depressed I actually was behind my mask, it would have been a complete shock. I was just the happy go-lucky girl who liked dolphins and laughed a lot. So again, just like Eve, I hid.

In a not-so-spiritual sense, my shame hit its peak one morning in a hotel room in LA. I woke up, stomach burning and head pounding, grabbed a bottle of rum next to my bed, and just stared. With my eyes glassed over and the room spinning, I stared at that bottle like it was my only way out. That bottle was my one ticket to escape from myself. I held it up, counted my losses in my head, and broke down on the ground. Laying there, hating everything that I was, all I could think about wanting to do with that bottle was finish it off in hopes of either forgetting about life for a while, or maybe even just being done all together. That may have been the darkest moment of my life. It was the first time I had genuinely entertained the idea of wanting to take my own life. Earlier that night, my boss and I had continued doing the usual, but this time it was in the same hotel that my sister was staying in as well. Literally two floors apart. It was sick, and I felt disgusting. But it was too late. The phone alarms went off and another day had to begin.

Reminiscing back on that night in the hotel, the saddest part of it all was the voluntary prison that I kept myself in. I stayed trapped for many reasons, but one in particular that breaks my heart the most today was my codependent attachment to this person. The closer we would get, the more emotional pain I would feel watching him flirt with other girls and such the next day. But why did it bother me so much? I knew I could never be with him, I knew I wasn't even supposed to let the mistakes that kept happening, happen. There was even a small part of me that felt an anger towards this guy that I had never felt before, and I didn't know exactly why. But somehow my heart was now involved, and I wanted to do my absolute best to never let that become known. I didn't want him to know that I was hurting, I didn't want him to know my heart was involved because

I had never had a good experience with that kind of vulnerability before. So I just pretended not to care.

The longer this went on, the less of an accident it felt like. It got to the point where I would come over late at night to help him with work, but as soon as I walked in the door, the work would stop and it turned into the same cycle of nonsense. We both knew what was going to happen, but neither one of us would put it to an end.

But if I knew how much this made me hate myself, why in the world was I okay with it? I very well remembered how much shame I was about to feel the next morning. Why did I continue to choose to partake in it? I even remember flat out telling him I wasn't hurting. I would say, "well, all my friends are doing it, so I'm sure it's normal and I'll be okay."

I didn't know it then, but now the answer is so obvious and simple that I wish I could go back in time and yell it in my 19-year-old face. The shame that started to develop that first morning on the bus grew into a complete devaluing of myself, and a self hatred that I would have never admitted, no matter who asked. I never spoke up because I was scared. I never gave anyone the opportunity to see my broken pieces and show me love anyway. I never gave myself the opportunity to experience the grace that I so desperately needed to survive. I stayed hidden and isolated, and continued to hate myself enough to let myself be used. If I didn't respect myself, why should he? Why should anyone? My heart naturally craved love and connection, and I thought that this was the only way I would ever get it, because somehow I thought that it was all that I deserved. That's why I was so scared to get out of it. Without this version of love, no matter how twisted it was, I didn't think I would be loved at all.

Trauma

"Because nobody goes through life without a scar."

– Carol Burnett

I'VE HEARD IT A MILLION TIMES, ODDS ARE YOU have too, that we tend to be our own hardest critics. It's pretty ironic how it works, but the scary truth behind it is that, well, it's reality.

The term "worthless" is a very bold statement to put on someone, nonetheless yourself. What is it that truly can make a person claim that as a part of who they are? Is it the class you failed, the guy that broke your heart, the dad that left you, the religion you can't keep up with? Hey, you know what, all those reasons are valid. All those reasons, or any other for that matter are real and they make complete sense. Things happen in this world that make us feel broken. They cause us to be blinded to who we are, and all we can feel is our value going away. We all have a story that might tell us that about ourselves. But let me just tell you right now that if you're reading this and you know what it feels like to seem unlovable, worthless, stupid, etc., I want to tell you that those words are straight up bald-faced lies. I promise you that the second you are actually able to stop believing them to be true, it will feel as if burdens have physically lifted from your shoulders. Those lies only keep us from seeing the beauty in who we actually are, and who we're truly created to be. They make us believe that we're garbage which in return makes us act that way, then try to cover it up. Silence only makes those words louder. A close friend told me once that when we speak up, the enemy can't. That is one of the incredible truths I've experienced that has changed my life. If there's something that you've done, or something that has happened to you that has made these lies define you, please don't hide. Please don't shove them to the cold back rooms of your heart and let them sit in isolation. As Christa Black says, "Unhealed pain never goes away on it's own."

Sometimes the answer to killing the silence about these lies is to speak up about them to a close friend or two, and sometimes it involves talking to a pastor or counselor. That's been my experience anyway, I've attempted all of the above. I am a slightly different case at times, considering most of my life is on the internet. Sometimes I meet people and they tell me how much they love my videos, and my stomach drops and my mind begins racing with thoughts of, *"wait, which video did you watch? What do you know?"*

All I'm saying is that keeping quiet about the lies you are hearing is never the answer. Talking it out is how we can find out what's true and what's not, and honestly, if the response you're getting is coming from God or someone who genuinely does love Jesus, I guarantee you will be pleasantly surprised with how encouraging the truth about who you are actually is. You might even become convinced that sharing how you're feeling isn't such a scary thing after all.

There are a lot of stories that I could tell you that would explain how I got stuck feeling how I did about myself back then. I was ridiculously insecure, not saying that I've got it all figured out now or anything crazy like that, but being at the point of darkness that I was at had to have come from somewhere. Everyone has a story. Everyone has a reason for being the way that they are. It's up to us to take the time to learn that story rather than judge, ignore, and assume the worst.

There were plenty of mean kids along the way, failures in sports, or screw-ups in school that could have created this identity for me. I was even labeled someone's "back up best friend" for a while, for crying out loud! And to make matters even worse, I was excited about that title because it meant that I was that much closer to having a best friend. But how did it get that bad? How did I get to the point of questioning whether or not I wanted to exist anymore?

~~~

When I was 17-years-old, I was raped. Getting that sentence out has, for some reason, been both one of my biggest struggles, and greatest victories. I don't know why but when I try to talk about this with people, getting out the word "raped," or even "molested," feels almost impossible. I feel like I can actually taste how disgusting it sounds when I say it, so most of the time when I try to tell my story, I either skip it or awkwardly whisper what happened with a weirdly obnoxious smile on my face. Sometimes I even insinuate what I'm trying to say, ask if the person I'm talking to gets the point of where I'm going, then I just jump to the end. Confused? Most likely.

Why is that? Even when I talk about it with people who get it and have been through it, that word seems untouchable and I have no idea why. Whenever I try to tell my story to a friend or someone in my family, that part stresses me out to the point of tears. I don't know if it's because of shame, fear, embarrassment, or trust, but it's unfortunately been a really rare thing for me to talk about in the past. The reason I use the word "unfortunate" is because keeping quiet about these things is probably the worst thing we can ever do. When we don't speak up, the enemy has free range. I believe that is why the quieter we are about these things, the worse we feel.

I think one reason I don't like telling people is because part of me is scared that I'll come off as *overly dramatic*. I have this strange fear that my problems and my story will become burdensome to people I share them with, and everyone will freak out and feel like they have to fix me or something. Then it will get to be too intense, I'll be too much to handle, and people will leave. Let me tell you, there are not a lot of things out there that feel as painful as the people you were vulnerable with leaving. I guess those are just my fears, and all they've done is keep me isolated.

On top of that, I have, for some reason, felt like I had to put a smile on my face through the pain for the majority of my life. I grew up hearing the phrase, "there's no crying in baseball," as if it was meant to be my life motto. And being rewarded when I sucked it up and didn't cry for things like getting hit in the head or falling off my bike didn't help either. I had scrapes and scars for days, but tears were constantly kept at a minimum. I was told that being tough was a good thing, and showing any sort of pain made me a wuss. Even writing this out right now is bringing so much clarity to why I pretend to be okay when I'm not. But I'm sick of doing that, so I'm going to try to stop. I'm not saying that I'm going to bawl my eyes out every time I stub my toe (even though that's a completely under-stated amount of pain and valid reason for anyone to bawl their eyes out), I'm just going to start living life knowing that when I feel real pain, it's okay to show it.

Every day I learn a little bit more about the power of shar-ing our stories, but the most I was ever impacted by it was when a friend of mine that I had just met openly shared that she was raped. I couldn't believe how open she was, and how she owned what hap-pened to her instead of letting what happened own her. It was hon-estly not even slightly expected, we were just in a group of trusted young women and she decided to own her story and share it. She shared it because she felt free. She shared it because she knew it had power. I had never witnessed something like that before. I had never had the opportunity to talk about what happened to me with someone who understood, because I never had the courage to boldly bring it up in that way.

I prayed in my head while she shared her story. I asked Jesus to help me. I needed courage to speak up and go to her. This was my chance! I needed the freedom that she had. *"Jesus, if she's some-one I need to share my story with, please make it easy and obvious. Please provide an opportunity for me to this where I don't even have to question whether it's right or not."* That was my prayer. Following my prayer, she asked me to help carry the food from our group into her office. Arms full of chip bags and paper plates, I followed her into her office and the door closed behind me. Alone in the office with just her and a trash can full of half eaten chips, there was my answered prayer. So as usual, face and palms a sweaty mess, I put on the biggest cheesiest grin and quietly coughed up my story.

By my friend choosing to speak boldly about her story, it then became a key that set me free. Strangely, for the first time I realized that I'm not alone, and if people like me continue to keep quiet about these things, we're going to keep others from feeling the same freedom as well. My friend is a world changer. Thank you for sharing your story. Thank you to all of you.

That's why I want to share this part of my story with you. If you're out there reading this and have gone through rape, sexual assault, or anything remotely similar you are so far from anything close to being alone.

~

When I was 15, I met who I thought was going to be my ride-or-die, best friend forever, adopted big sister, and so on. She was exactly who I thought I needed to feel valuable. For the purpose of this book, we'll call her Suzy. Suzy was a little older than me, and was practically the definition of controlling, manipulative, and painfully cool all at the same time. She knew what she wanted and she knew how to get it. No matter how many people saw that in her and warned me, and there were a lot, I didn't buy into it. I was loyal to Suzy and just thrilled to have a best friend as cool as I thought she was. Like I've said before, having a best friend or big sister like on the Disney Channel was the dream for me. It was what I thought I needed to feel loved and valued, so I made the decision to stick around with her.

Suzy and I were pretty much inseparable. We got our nails done together, went grocery shopping together, I'd hide at her house when I'd fight with my parents or sister, and so on. She was the first person to ever tell me what unconditional love meant, right after she claimed to love me that way. So I told her everything there was to know about me. Closer than any other friend I'd ever had, I let Suzy really deep into my life. I thought she was the best friend I would ever have and I would have done just about anything to make her happy. This involved multiple occasions of me paying for her gas, food, phone bill, and even hair appointments. If there was someone in my life that Suzy didn't like, I got rid of them. There was even a time when a boy I liked dropped off a bouquet of roses on my doorstep but since Suzy didn't like him, she asked me to shut him down. So I did. Suzy was the one who got me into the Rebel Jackie days. I remember it like it was yesterday, sitting next to her while I smoked my first bowl of weed, ironically in a church parking lot, which started what I call my "stoner years." Honestly, I didn't care. I just wanted to be liked and be approved of and she was the one who I gave the place in my life to do that.

Two years into our friendship, Suzy started dating this guy that we can refer to as Josh. Things with those two got serious pretty fast, and Suzy ended up moving in and then getting pregnant a few months later. My role as the best friend then translated into attending doctors appointments, paying for her food, gas, baby things, and basically everything else inbetween. Josh, Suzy, and I ended up becoming like a little family throughout this season and were even looking into getting an apartment all together to save money. We had a folder of listings printed off the internet, budgets sorted out, you name it. They were my family, I was going to be Aunty Jackie and I thought I was in it to help them for the long run.

Then one day I got a phone call. I had never gotten one like this before, only heard about them from friends or on TV. It was a phone call that lead to me ditching school, jumping in my car, and, without a second thought heading straight to the hospital. Suzy was going to lose the baby. I sat there in the waiting room in pure shock. I had never experienced something like this before. I had never been around death in this close of vicinity, much less not for people that I was this close to. The pain in the room was loud. The fear in the room felt heavy. Family members of both Suzy and Josh that I had never met before surrounded me in the room. Holding their faces deep within their hands as if it was the one place they could find sanctuary, no one said a word.

After experiencing about five minutes of life on this cold, sad day, Suzy's baby died right there in her arms.

She continued to hold her, almost as if it was just easier to pretend she was still there. It was as if postponing reality was another option, a better one for that matter. I have never felt more helpless, more unable to speak than I did that day. They asked me to hold the baby, so I reached out and cradled that tiny little human with more heart ache than I could put words to. Looking at the baby's tightly wrapped body was more of a burden than I could bare, so I closed my eyes and silently rocked her back and forth. Silence was long and loud, and words felt meaningless.

When trauma happens, everyday life just isn't as simple as it once was. The person left with the broken pieces has a choice to make: face the pain and search for healing, or numb out. Numbing out from trauma could be something as innocent as watching tv shows, to as serious as overdosing on drugs. Suzy coped by locking herself in her room, and Josh handled his trauma by numbing out with alcohol.

It was about two weeks after the hospital visits that the day began that changed the course of my life. Not like I knew it though, I woke up and went to work just like any other day. I was a host at a steakhouse back then. Not too similar to the taco place I'm at today, but I truly did love working there. It was a place where I felt like I belonged, a place where I could bring a fart machine to work and hide it under the host stand without getting into too much trouble. However it was also a place where I got written up for dancing at the host stand with my friend Mariah. My friend Abbie used to find it hysterical to draw pictures of dolphins saying, "I hate Jackie," and put them all over the restaurant. I had mixed emotions sometimes, but we got free honey cinnamon bread every night so it wasn't all that bad. Free carbs would make anyone want to work somewhere, if you ask me.

Josh also worked at the steakhouse with me. He got off a little bit before I did that night and sat down with some other servers to drink about three margaritas. They all had plans to go to a bar that night and Josh wanted to go too but needed a DD since he was already pretty drunk, so he asked me to do it. This guy was like my big brother, which is what he called himself and what his name was in my phone. Of course I would help. Pulling out of the parking lot at work, he kept calling me "little sis" and thanking me for being such a great friend.

Once we got to the bar I didn't see Josh again until closing time. There were so many people there, and being only 17, I wasn't really involved in much of the fun. I ended up killing time playing pool with some other servers, sitting by myself at a table texting Suzy, or sparking up random conversations with the drunk bar crowd. I had never been to a bar before like this and didn't really know what my place was.

Last call came, and Josh was ready to be driven home. We left the bar but he decided that he wanted to stop at Walmart for something to drink before we went home. Things started to get weird. He forced me into the passenger seat to let him drive, defeating the purpose of me being there in the first place. He drove me around the block a few times, then began telling me about dreams that he had been having about me. I sat silent. We left walmart, walked back to the car, and he opened up the door to the back seat to pick me up and put me inside. That's when it began. I would argue and tell him no, and he would put his hand over my mouth and tell me to shut up. I was terrified. That was the night that would from then on out affect me for the rest of my life.

I want to pause this story for a moment and speak to those of you out there reading this who have been through this before. There's a possible chance that hearing my story brought up some things that you've put off to the side, or triggered some shame and fear from somewhere in your past. I want to speak to you and tell you that you are loved, and that everything that you're feeling right now is valid and important and if you shared your story with someone, it would be an honor for them to be there for you in this. I want to let you know that there is light on the other side. In fact, typing the words to this story was surprisingly easy for me today. It's actually the first time I've felt this thick of a layer of healing from this trauma, and I want that in itself to encourage you that the pain you're feeling now is not forever. It's scary and it's isolating because who's going to ever truly understand? Who would ever want to carry such a burden with me? Who would know what to say? Those were my thoughts at least. Those were also my lies that I believed. The moment that I realized I was worth protecting was the moment that I shared, and the moment that Jesus showed me where he was when this was happening.

I don't know who you are, I don't know if you believe in Jesus or not, but I can tell you that because of the healing that I received from this alone, I know that there is a God and that he loves me. I also know that he is not a God that makes bad things happen. I know that we live in a world full of hate, lies, and evil, and *that* is why these bad things happen. But I also know that because there is a God, we can overcome that world and all the evil in it. I experienced that overcoming from this story in itself.

~

Depending on your personal beliefs, this next part of my story might sound a little crazy to you, but bare with me here because what I want to share next with you was honestly one of the most pivotal moment in my life, and the idea of not sharing it does not make any sense.

As I closed my eyes for worship just barely a year ago, Jesus showed me where he was when I was raped. Clear as day, I saw the whole scene as if I was there reliving it and feeling terrified all over again. There I was in the backseat of Josh's car, when suddenly I saw a hand reach in and pull me out. Holding me and weeping, we sat outside. But it wasn't just teary eyed weeping, it was full on hysterics. It was the kind of crying that a dad would do if his daughter was the one experiencing this trauma. It was as if he was feeling this pain with me. I wasn't alone. Jesus was there with me and he held me in his arms because sometimes when we're going through hell, the only way we can find peace is in his presence. Sometimes words don't always fix things. Don't get me wrong, the power in words is truly life changing. But I was told by a friend once that sometimes when we're at our lowest points, we get to know a whole different side of Jesus. It sucks, to be honest, because it takes going through hell to get there but once we do, it'll never be the same. That side of Jesus is a side that has no words. It's a side of Jesus that sees where we are, validates that, and just simply holds us.

I wish I could say that this healing was instant. I wish I could say that right after the rape, I woke up the next morning and Jesus was showing me these things and crying with me and the healing began. But it didn't. At the time of my abuse, I didn't know Jesus yet. It actually wasn't until two years later that that happened, so unfortunately it was a pretty bumpy road until the true healing began.

I got home that night at about 4 AM. I walked upstairs, locked myself in my bathroom, took off my clothes, and stared at my underwear. This stillness that I felt was new territory that my body had never experienced before. It was so still that it didn't seem real. Did that actually happen? Did I just imagine that? I felt like I had to force myself to breathe as if it no longer came naturally.

I didn't want to sit in that for one second longer so I threw my underwear away and forced myself to go to sleep. The next morning I remember waking up on the couch, and I honestly have no idea how I got there because, as far as I can remember, I fell asleep on the bathroom floor. A phone call from Josh is what woke me up. Dazed and confused, still in somewhat of a denial at what just happened, I answered the phone. Hoping it was all just a dream, yet at the same time expecting some sort of answers to what I was feeling, all he did was ask, "What's this giant bottle of Sprite doing in my front seat?" I asked him if he remembered anything from the night before and, to this day, I can't decide if his response of blacking out was the truth or not. It was at that moment that I realized I was the only person in the whole world who knew what had happened to me. I hung up the phone, my back slammed against the wall as I slid to the floor in tears, wishing I didn't exist. I've never felt more alone than I did in that moment. I had a decision to make. Do I tell someone what happened? Do I pretend nothing happened? Is that even possible? I was scared, I was confused, and I was very, very alone.

―――〰――――

I tend to consider myself as generally a pretty vulnerable person. I'm not saying that it's easy and natural for me to share the depths of my heart on a daily basis, it actually took an extremely long time for me to finally reach this level of transparency with, not only people, but even myself about how I'm feeling.

Growing up I was the girl who choked back the tears when I got hit in the face with a baseball, on multiple occasions, out of fear of being seen as weak or girly. However today, I believe I'm practically an open book with most people. I mean, come on, like I said earlier, my whole life is on the internet, for crying out loud! So, if that's the case, if my heart's desire is to create a safe environment for people to share their authentic selves, if I preach how important vulnerability is on a daily basis, why do I still hide from the fact that I was raped? When I share my story with people on how I met Jesus or how I got from point A to point B in my life, why is the one event that I hate sharing being sexually assaulted by my best friend's boyfriend? Why is that a story that I never even felt comfortable telling my own dad about?

The rape culture in today's world is a scary, frustrating thing. Statistics show that one in every four women experience sexual abuse in their lifetime. That's a lot of broken hearts. That's a lot of hurting, abused women who most likely feel as if they're now defected, dirty, and unlovable. At least, that's how I felt. But if there are that many cases of this happening, why do we feel so alone in it? Why do we feel like speaking up is next to impossible? As for my story, the bar was set pretty low for how responses went right from the start.

One of the first people I had to tell my story to when my best friend's boyfriend raped me was, well, my best friend. But, just so we're clear, as obvious as it was that she needed to know, I was pretty confident in my original idea of shoving it under a rug and never letting her, or really anyone for that matter, in. As crazy at it feels now to even imagine me going the rest of my life not telling anyone, it seemed like the safest option at the time. Calling Suzy that night to tell her what had happened easily ranks as one of the top three scariest conversations I've ever had. Isn't that sad? Isn't your best friend supposed to be your no matter what, bury-the-body-with-you type of person that knows your heart and soul better than anybody else in the whole world? At least, that's what I learned by watching Disney Channel all my life, or pretty much any other tv show or movie for that matter. The reason I was so scared to let my best friend in on what happened was because this put her in the position to make a choice, and I desperately feared that her choice would not be me. Why didn't I think she would choose me? The answer is the same as why I didn't tell my dad what happened either. I didn't see myself as valuable in literally the slightest bit. I wasn't valuable enough to be chosen, and I wasn't valuable enough to be protected.

Two days later, I was in Florida on vacation with my aunt and big sister. Some vacation, huh? I got on the plane and felt like my heart stayed behind in Colorado. I felt numb. My heart wasn't a safe place anymore, and neither was my body. I felt like they no longer belonged to me. But honestly one of the scariest things is that there was still a part of me that was convinced I had made it all up. There was also a part of me that felt like it was all my fault. Then I'd step back into reality and feel the physical pain down my back and in my stomach, and realize the new trauma that made its home in my heart. I just wanted to disappear all together. Everything around me suddenly felt like the potential of an escape. Maybe the car I was in could crash, the food I was eating could choke me, the creepy man at the next table could be a terrorist; it didn't matter, and as hard as it feels now to admit, any of those escapes would have been fine with me. I just wanted out.

I knew what needed to be done, so after hours of working up enough courage to even get the words out to myself in a mirror, I called my best friend. I sat on this dock by the restaurant we were at, distanced myself from my heart, and I dialed her number. She answered, and I froze. I couldn't get a word out so she just started yelling at me to tell her what happened. I swallowed my fear, slammed the door shut on my emotions, clenched my fists, and began to share my story. "*He raped me.*" The only thing that came next was silence. No one said a word. She didn't ask if I was okay, she didn't tell me she cared about me or was sorry about what happened. Next thing I knew she started screaming and hung up the phone. I liked the silence better. Again, my body froze. I felt myself stand up and walk to the bathroom, kind of like an out of body experience. I couldn't even look in the mirror, all I felt was this fear for how worthless I must be. If my own best friend didn't believe me, nobody would. If my own best friend didn't see me as valuable enough to care about, nobody would. A few hours later she called me back. Pacing back and forth outside the hotel room, I slowly swallowed the lump in my throat and answered the phone. "*Jackie, are you sure you didn't want it to happen? I mean you were drinking too.*" And just like that, I hung up the phone. She stayed with him, and never spoke another word to me again.

Little Sister

"God is going to reveal me as a flawed human being as fast as he can and he's going to enjoy it because it will force me to grapple with real intimacy."

– Donald Miller

WHEN I WAS 19, I PACKED UP MY CAR AND moved my life from Colorado to LA. Moving to California had been this long lost childhood dream of mine for practically as long as I can remember. We went out there all the time growing up, and I fell in love. I was loud and proud about wanting to move there as early as seven years old, so the fact that I did still impresses me, if I do say so myself. I'm sure you're all assuming that I wanted to pursue acting or singing or some form of getting famous. If you didn't assume that, I apologize for jumping to conclusions, that's just what 90% of the people I tell my story to assume. Fame was never my intention, my dream was to be a dolphin trainer. No joke! That's what I've been known for practically my whole life. I even went to this thing called Dolphin Camp in Florida once, which always gives people a nice little chuckle when they find out that I'm not making it up.

It all started when I was about six years old at Sea World. I was at the dolphin petting area and, as I was laying across the wall on my little belly, a dolphin came up and brought me a feather. So I took the feather and threw it, which started a pleasant game of fetch for a solid two minutes. I remember this story vividly, partially because it was truly a life altering event, and partially because I wrote about it in my six year old diary. Anyway, that's the fun fact I use during ice breakers and random awkward social gatherings, that's the story I tell when I want someone to think I'm unique, and that's the dream that convinced me to pack up my car and head west. Not to mention, it seemed like a perfectly good time as any to start my life over.

I wish I could leave it there and blame the dolphins for my sudden change of scenery, but since this book is meant to be vulnerable and honest to the core, I guess that leaves me obligated to tell you the other truth behind why I moved, no matter how pathetic it might make me look. On top of wanting to be paid to hang out with sea animals all day, I really just wanted to run. After what happened to me when I was 17, I had felt like I'd been constantly running from something and I didn't know what it was. Now it's easy to look back and pinpoint the fact that I was running from myself, my pain, my trauma... but back then it didn't feel that simple. It was my assumption that if I moved to another state and surrounded myself with all new people and brand new things, the pain would disappear. So as soon the first semester of my attempted college dorm experience was over, I split.

My sister was living in LA at the time doing music with her boyfriend. Remember that guy I was talking about at the beginning of all this nonsense? Yep, that's the one. For the book's purpose, we'll refer to him as Steve. I don't know a Steve right now, but if I happen to meet one down the road after this book is published, I apologize for any confusion and inconvenience that I just added to your life. Sorry, Steve. I'm sure you're a great guy.

Anyway, at this point in my life, all I wanted was a relationship with my big sister, and this seemed like my shot. I wanted that so desperately for the majority of my life growing up, but this time in particular was very unique. As I've said multiple times, I let Disney Channel define what I thought life was supposed to look like. Therefore, I wanted a relationship with my sister to look like Lizzie and Miranda or Miley and Lilly. Anything close to that would've been just fine. I thought that if I had that one thing, I would be okay. That's where I thought my healing and identity would come from. That's where I thought I would find my purpose.

Before I moved to LA, I would sit in my dorm at night just waiting for my sister to call me back. I would post a photo on Instagram and constantly check to see if she had liked it yet, because most of the time I was posting hoping she would see it and think I was cooler than I actually was. I used to talk about Alex to all my friends as if we were best friends. Since she did music, most of the people who knew me ended up finding out about her and obsessing as well. She would be a popular topic, so I felt like I needed her approval even more now in order to gain my friend's as well.

There were two friends of mine, however, that never once made me feel that way. These are pretty much the only two friends that I actively keep in touch with from my high school days, and really get to hang out with on a semi-regular basis. Well, as regular as it can be living states apart anyway. Sehler (like a sailor on a ship) has been like a brother to me for almost twelve years now, ever since the day I met him in Mrs. Nelson's social studies class and he was talking about Nintendogs and his Nintendo DS. He's the one that I would call late at night to help me figure out how to beat Super Mario Sunshine, or stay up talking about the band we were going to make until seven in the morning called "The Trolly Dodgers." He's also the one who I used to make music videos with and post them on YouTube. Go check, they're still there. Then there's Sydney. Sydney has been my "soulmate," as we like to say, since I was a junior in high school. She's the one that I started a corn dog club with, and the one who I spontaneously bought a hamster named Topanga with one day after we were on our way home from watching buffalos hang out. She's the one that I would always look out for me when we would end up at some weird party where we were scared they were smoking meth or something. I don't think they were smoking meth, but Sydney had my back either way. In her words, "A good friend is someone who makes sure you don't accidentally smoke meth." If you make friends like Sehler and Sydney, hold onto them.

Anyway, looking back at it now, I can honestly say that Alex and I didn't know each other much at all. I hadn't lived in the same house as her for a few years now, so I still knew her as the softball playing, Guitar Hero winning 17-year-old girl that I shared a bathroom with, and she knew me as the rolly pollie-collecting little kid who always stole her clothes. When I say "always," I mean always. Hollister was a big deal to most of us back then so her wardrobe was a necessity, in my defense. But no, I didn't know what made Alex, Alex, and she didn't know what made me, me. It actually got a little awkward at times when I moved out there. We didn't spend a whole lot of time together just the two of us, but when we did, it normally looked like us constantly listening to her different demos from her album on repeat in the car to avoid the awkward silences. We ended up going to Universal Studios together one time and were next up in line to ride this ride that I was secretly scared of, and instead of telling her I didn't want to go, I just pretended I had to go to the bathroom so I needed to leave. That's how uncomfortable I was around her. I would have rather make her think I had to pee than tell her how I actually felt. She still rode the ride alone though, so props to her for that. I was too scared.

However, even with all of that weirdness, I still desperately longed for my sister's attention. I wanted to be loved and accepted by her more than anything else in the world. I wanted that because, in my head, I thought that unless I had it, I would never be good enough. I thought she was the standard. Looking back now, it's obvious that the root issue there was a painful codependency problem, but at the time it was real to me and I was determined to make it happen. Since I would be moving in with her, I thought this was my chance to get her to like me. I did everything I could in preparation for my move to make that happen. As embarrassing as this is to put in my book, I'll tell you that I learned how to cook Alex's favorite meals, I got new clothes that would make me look cool and "LA," I practiced filming and editing; everything that I could think of that would make me of more use to her in LA, I did.

When we were growing up, Alex and I went back and forth with liking each other one day and getting on each other's last nerve the next. As little kids we would put on plays and musicals in the basement, and danced around to *Hairspray* and *High School Musical*

CDs. We would put all our dress up clothes on and pretend we were performing, getting every bit of it on tape as we could. We would play with Polly Pockets and Barbies for days. Literally, *for days*. There were multiple occasions of us having a storyline all set up for our Barbies and when we would be done playing for the day, we would leave them exactly where they were so we could pick them up the next day where they left off. Then she eventually outgrew that, which left me playing by myself. That was one of the saddest moments of my eight year old life. Remember that scene in *Frozen* when Anna would knock on Elsa's door, begging her to come out and play but was constantly rejected? Yeah that was me. As I'm assuming most sibling relationships go, the older we would get, the more conflict would occur, and not just about me stealing her Hollister jeans. As I got older, I started to make friends with people that my sister didn't exactly approve of. She didn't approve of my Rebel Jackie lifestyle one little bit, and even woke me up in the middle of the night crying because she found out that I had been smoking weed after reading through my texts. That was the roughest it had gotten between us at that point in time, and my Rebel Jackie friends couldn't stand her either. She really didn't like me at this time in my life, but I still deep down really wanted her to.

I think part of the reason I wanted her approval so bad was because, in the public's eye, it seemed like Alex was perfect. It seemed like she had it all together.Like, both of her socks matched on a daily basis sort of thing and she knew what to do and where to go in life. She was great at school, great at sports, and once that whole YouTube music career took off, it just seemed obvious that her life was going places. Slowly but surely she became my standard for what cool was, and that's just about as unhealthy for both of us as it gets. I mean I had relatives calling me on the phone telling me that I should drop everything I was doing, all my goals and dreams, and just start an Alex G fanclub. I was told by my own family members that to be smart I needed to, "hang onto my sister's coat tails because she's really going places." I'm not making this stuff up. Kids at school that at first wanted nothing to do with me, now wanted to be my best friend because my sister was on YouTube and, "her 'Cups' cover was really good." During the holidays, the main talk was about Alex's music and who she was doing her next video with. It got to the point that even Alex was getting sick of talking about herself. Now that I think about it, I actually feel pretty bad for little Alex back then. I don't know what it's like to struggle with perfectionism, but seeing what she went through, I can't even imagine what kind of pressure she probably felt to perform. Anyway, all of this stuff was doing nothing but making me feel like I needed to be more and more like my sister, and less and less like me.

So there I was, first day in the big city, all excited about my fresh start! I was nervous and excited and so ready for the new. When I pulled up to her apartment, she wasn't there. She told me she would be. She actually told me to come on that specific day because it was the only one that worked for her at the time. So I showed up, but she wasn't there. Hour after hour went by, and finally she called me back. She was headed back to her spot so my excitement built up and I went to meet her. I had been walking around downtown all day killing time, applying for jobs, and doing my best not to get lost in my new city. I found my way back to her apartment and she hopped in my car. The first thing she did was ask me to take her to the airport.

Completely caught off guard and heart crushed, I sat there silent as Alex told me that she had a free flight back home to Colorado and chose to use it that day, the day she told me to come, to go surprise Steve who had just moved back to Colorado a couple days before. I didn't want to risk making her upset, so I swallowed the dagger I felt like just hit me in the face and I drove her to the airport. I got back to her apartment complex, sat in my car and just cried. I cried so hard and I didn't even know the words to put to the pain, all I knew was it was there. Feeling rejected, worthless, and alone, I was in LA and I was scared. I barely knew her roommate at the time, and I was afraid that he wouldn't want to be around me either at this rate. I was scared he didn't even want me to live with him but there was no going back now, I left Colorado behind and was now committed to mov.ng forward with a life in LA. Sneaking into the apartment, hoping he wouldn't hear me come in, I hid in Alex's empty room and laid down on the floor and yes, I cried some more. I also ate a half eaten box of *I Love Lucy* themed chocolates which is irrelevant, but hey, at least I had that one going for me.

I Am the Problem

"We make loving people a lot more complicated than Jesus did."

– Bob Goff

WHEN I WAS 20, I WAS GIVEN THE BOOK *BLUE Like Jazz* by Donald Miller for Christmas. I didn't have the slightest idea how big of a day that was for me. I wasn't much of a reader at the time. Growing up I enjoyed anything having to do with puppies, Lizzie McGuire, or *A Series of Unfortunate Events* by Lemony Snicket, but nothing past that. This is a total side note, but in fifth grade I was so determined to read Lizzie McGuire yet so scared my friends would think I was a loser for reading it that I hid it inside of a bigger book in school so no one would know. However, being 20 and all, I felt like as an official grown up I should probably consider picking up an actual novel that wasn't based off the Disney Channel. After finishing the book in about two weeks, it was a pretty quick realization that I now needed to devour every word Donald Miller has ever and will ever write. Needless to say I had my first favorite author.

When I was 22, I met Donald Miller in an elevator. Technically it was outside of the elevator, but I was too nervous to take specific scenic notes, so bare with me here. He walked out, looked my way, and I froze.

"Are you Donald Miller?"

"Yes, I am! Who are you?"

"I'm Jackie!" (As if he totally should have known that already after how much time I spent reading about his life).

That pretty much sums up our conversation. Don, if you have for some incredible reason decided to read my book, you should know that I really enjoyed our deep and extensive lifechat by the elevator.

⌒

"Nothing is going to change in the congo until you and I figure out what is wrong with the person in the mirror."

Out of the hours I've spent reading about Don's life, listening to his podcasts, chatting with him by elevators, and begging my friends to read the stacks of books I have by him in my room, this quote from *Blue Like Jazz* might be one of the most impactful things I've ever come across by him. There comes a time in every person's life, or at least there came one in mine, when political and social issues in the world have to stop being ignored. I grew up in a very loud political environment. The people around me were, at least in my opinion, pretty obnoxious and a bit cruel when it came to political conversations. As I started to grow up and go to school, I wouldn't hear anything different from the kids around me either. Then I'd get on the internet for a minute and it just got worse, believe it or not. (Hopefully my sarcasm is picked up here. I'm used to rant-ing about these things while talking in a video instead of in writing.) That being said, my method of survival from the numerous political debates became tuning it out. Literally all of it. It got so bad that I didn't even know who was running for president, nor did I want to. It was like an alarm went off in my brain, warning my ears to stop working for a second when I sensed a comment about "the liberals" was potentially approaching.

This lasted until about two hours before the voting polls closed last November. With every intention of ignoring the countless peo-ple nagging me to vote, something inside me couldn't let myself also ignore the pain behind the people I was voting for. Thinking about it in that light, it didn't seem as simple to avoid. So there I was in my car, texting everyone I could remember who had nagged me from both sides of the political parties asking them to resend the articles and videos that they had already sent me multiple times but didn't survive the delete button. I had about two hours of poll time left, and I was planning on using that time to anxiously go back and relearn everything that I had been tuning out for the past 21 years.

After those two hours came to an end, I started to learn some-thing and it wasn't that the democrats were evil and the republicans are the best and right about everything, or vice versa. I know there's most likely people reading this right now crossing their fingers and biting their tongues, waiting for me to say something mean about one political party or the other, but you're probably going to be dis-appointed, so I might as well let you down with that now. This isn't that kind of book. If that's what you're looking for, go look pretty much anywhere else on the internet and you won't be disappointed.

That day, I learned that I am the problem. Not the democrats, not the liberals, and not the conservatives; me. It was obvious who was on whose side on Facebook. It was obvious what kind of phrases or hashtags I could have used to look supportive of the side my friends were on, or the cute boy I wanted to like me. But what was that going to do? I could have easily posted some video or Instagram picture claiming to #LetLoveWin or #MakeAmericaGreatAgain, but would that have actually made a difference, or would that have just made me look like someone who's making a difference? If I marched in that protest, would I be helping someone, or would I be making myself look like someone who helps people?

In *Blue Like Jazz*, Don tells the story about the time when he went to a protest to hold up a sign to support a cause. He stood there among the other protesters, but couldn't stop thinking about the real reason he was there.

> *"More than my questions about the efficacy of social actions were my questions about my own motives. Do I want social justice for the oppressed or do I just want to be known as a socially active person? I spend 95 percent of my time thinking about myself anyway. I don't have to watch the evening news to see the world is bad, I only have to look at myself. I am not brow beating here, I am only saying that true change, true life giving, God honoring change would have to start with the individual. I was the very problem I had been protesting."*

I was at my restaurant job one night where I sold street style tacos in a blue and white checkered shirt I wasn't allowed to get my white pants dirty, when I had a moment. A couple sat down at one of my tables, and as I was filling up some water cups for them, I noticed one of the ladies pull out a few different t-shirts with different quotes on them about loving people. It made me smile and I was excited to go greet the table because I felt like they would probably be decent human beings which, believe it or not, are sometimes a rare thing to come by while working in the restaurant industry. I set down their trays and water cups with a big fat sweet little Jackie G smile and started to attempt a conversation with them. The details are pretty irrelevant at this point, but long story short these two ladies with the love t-shirts were the rudest table I had all night. They wouldn't look at me, they wouldn't respond to me, pretty much just treated me as their personal taco slave for the hour and a half that they occupied my table. In my opinion, they were there for an hour and a half too long.

It wasn't the fact that they were rude that made me mad. It wasn't even feeling like a taco slave that got to me because come one now, I was a waitress. Of course there were going to be people who I'd have to wait on that were going to feel entitled to the tacos. What really got to me were the t-shirts on display in front of the arrogance. Real problems occur when we are so focused on looking socially active, looking like we care about people, that we are blinded by the one thing we actually do have the power to make better; ourselves. That right there is my political view.

I think things like missions trips and charities and volunteering are great ideas. I think wanting to make the world a better place, raising money to feed the homeless, or traveling overseas to build someone a house is absolutely beautiful. But it becomes a tad bit confusing when the same people who are loud and proud about doing that can't even show love to the people next door. Those same people are flipping people off on the highway or leaving 8% tips when they go out to eat. What's that about?

So, in other words yes, I agree with you Don. "Nothing is going to change in the congo until you and I figure out what is wrong with the person in the mirror." Yes, I could wear that #LoveWins t-shirt. Yes, I could go on that mission trip or march in that parade and then throw it up on social media for everyone to see, but will I actually be brave enough to look in the mirror at myself and at my own relationships and come to terms with my own faults? Instead of pointing my finger at the hatred and cruelty in the world, will I have the courage to point my finger back at myself and look at where I've acted hateful or cruel? We've all been there. Hannah Montana was not just making a catchy pop jingle when she said that nobody's perfect.

Honestly, I believe that a big reason the world is such a scary place is because there are too many people who don't want to come to terms with their own brokenness. We're so quick to say, "Oh, well I would never do *that*!" or "At least I didn't do what *she* did…". But would you? There aren't a lot of things that I would say are braver than genuine self reflection. It's a scary, sad thing to do at times. I'm fully aware of that. But if we don't self reflect, if we don't look at our cracks straight in the mirror and see what we could actually do about it, we have nothing. Nobody is going to change somebody. My long political rant on Facebook isn't going to help anyone any more than the next person's. The only change we have the power of making is in our own lives. So before we start running around wearing shirts about love, how about we just actually love? Before we march in protests about treating people equally, why don't we start by saying hello to the man picking up the trash in the bathroom. Or are we too entitled for that? I realize that this is an extremely controversial subject. I realize that this section might make some people mad at me, but maybe I can use some more controversy in my life.

I have this friend that was telling me recently that she used to be told, "I don't know you love Jesus by you raising your hands in church, praying really long prayers, or posting selfies on Instagram with a Bible verse. I know that you love Jesus because of how you act. I know that you love Jesus because of how you treat people." If this girl never mentioned Jesus, I would still know that she loved him. I would still know that that's who she is because of how she treats people. If someone out there is upset, let's go take care of them. If someone needs a place to sleep, lets lend them a spot on the couch. If someone is hungry and doesn't have any food, why not buy them lunch? It's things like that that will make a difference in the world; actually loving people, not yelling at people to love people. Love is complicated, love is an action, and I don't think we represent it very well a lot of the time. But truthfully, at the end of the day, love is the greatest idea anyone has ever had. God is love, and that means that love is everything that God is. That means that love stands up for people, honors people, and respects people. Love is sacrificial. So if we want to know what love is, we have to know who God is.

New

"Because what else are we going to do? Say no to an opportunity that may be slightly out of our comfort zone? Quiet our voice because we are worried it is not perfect? I believe great people do things before they are ready."

– Amy Poehler

I TURNED 21 IN DECEMBER OF 2015. MY FRIENDS threw me a party at a beach house, so it wasn't too bad of a time. We played games, watched the sunrise, ate donuts, and had a grand old time. Not trying to brag, I'm just really proud of the fact that my friends are so awesome and that I got to live out an old childhood dream.

At my birthday party, my friend Lauren came up and told me, "Jackie, I feel like the word for your new year is going to be 'new.' It's going to be really new, really fast." I had absolutely no clue how right she would turn out to be.

As 2015 ended, one of the most intense years of my life thus far began. Well, every year has felt pretty intense in its own way, but there was something special about 2016 that just doesn't quite compare to the rest. You see, I closed off the year before living in LA, fully involved and committed at my church. I was leading a community group, had my favorite coffee shop to read in, and a Chipotle walking distance away, but something was not right. Remember that conversation I had to have with my sister? The one from the very beginning of this book? Well that secret life I had been living started to come to the surface to more than just her right as the new year began.

To be real with you guys, I am sometimes *still* so disappointed with the events that took place in January of 2016. That was the month that I desperately needed people. I needed my friends, my family, really anyone to be there for me and in a community of Christians and church folk, I didn't by any means expect this month to turn out the way that it did. Everyone has been stabbed in the back at least once in their life, so I'm sure someone out there can understand what I was feeling at this time.

January was a turning point in my life. The shame and trauma from my past were now coming to the surface, and I was dealing with them the best I knew how. I was done hiding my past. I didn't want to lie anymore, I didn't want to feel broken anymore, and I was sick and tired of being terrified that I was going to hell. As I've talked about countless times on YouTube, thoroughly in and through this book and so on, the way out of your shame is primarily only possible with people. Sharing your story with people is key. Letting people know you to the fullest extent can be the most healing thing in the whole world. But the people that I trusted to let in on my heart and my story through it all, let's just say that it did not go over well. Lies, rumors, loss of friendships, more confrontational conversations and unnecessary group interventions than I can even try to explain took place. I was kicked out of my Bible study, asked to leave my community group, received letters to end friendships that I greatly valued, and so on. It was hard and it was sad, and frankly one of the most lonely times of my life. I learned a lot though, as I'm assuming most people would in a situation like that. I learned how to tell if someone is either trustworthy or full of crap, I learned that sometimes the church doesn't do the best job at representing Jesus, and that just because a group of people pray really well and seem really spiritual doesn't mean you can trust them with your stuff. I learned that sometimes complete vulnerability does not go over very well, and that learning to be vulnerable again takes time and is anything but easy. It's interesting how when conflict hits a group of people, true colors start to show. It starts to become painfully clear who cares and who doesn't. Real conflict is like a veil that gets lifted off and reveals the truth in people's hearts.

To put this in a simpler form, my biggest fears were realized in January of 2016. The story that I thought made me unloveable, actually seemed to do just that. The story that I was scared of sharing with people because I thought it would make them not want to be my friends anymore, did just that. I'm not even sure what story everyone heard, to be totally honest. I only told two people and, before I knew it, everybody and their mom seemed to be cutting me out of their lives. I felt like Emma Stone in Easy A. Thus began "the great divide," as we refer to it today. Girls talk, I guess.

"No, life cannot be understood flat on a page. It has to be lived; a person has to get out of his head, has to fall in love, has to memorize poems, has to jump off bridges into rivers, has to stand in an empty desert and whisper sonnets under his breath... We get one story, you and I, and one story alone. God has established the elements, the setting and the climax and resolution. It would be a crime not to venture out, wouldn't it?"

– Donald Miller

So then what was next for me? There was no going back now, life was no longer going to be the same. I had a major loss of community, a new reputation that I did not like in the slightest bit, and no where to go. I remember this like it was yesterday. I was sitting on my bed in the middle of all this chaos. I was between the endless confrontational conversations I was being set up for, in the middle of mental breakdowns and anxiety attacks, and was simply just angry at this point. I was so over being sad, that mad seemed like a refreshing change of pace. I sat there on my bed and truly out of nowhere decided, "you know what? I'm just going to move to Nashville." That's what I would do! Forget all this garbage, forget these people, I wanted to be done. Why Nashville? No specific reason really, I just had this random love for that city that I didn't know what to do with. I didn't really know anyone there, I wasn't a musician, wasn't trying to go to Belmont, I just wanted out. That settled it! Almost...

About two minutes later reality kicked in and I realized that uprooting my life and leaving everything and everyone I knew behind without any reasoning behind it other than anger did not make a lot of sense. I couldn't just run away from my problems all over again, especially without the dolphin training excuse. However to be honest, I do sometimes tell people I moved to Nashville to be a dolphin trainer just for the confused look on their face and potential chuckle or two.

I took a deep breath, calmed myself down and I prayed. I prayed with everything I could, as hard as I knew how, and I asked Jesus for a sign. I asked him to give me such a specific sign that I should move to Nashville that I wouldn't even have to think twice about it.

Now, I've experienced answered prayers before, but to this day nothing has ever been able to compare to this one. That very night after I prayed that prayer, I went to church and started chatting with a good friend of mine. This was a friend who I loved dearly, but didn't know very well at the time. If I had only known how important this friend was about to become in my life, I wouldn't have known what to do. Halfway through the casual conversation, she started talking about her sister. Not thinking anything of it I just asked, "Oh, what does your sister do?" and she says, "Oh! She works at this ministry school that you would love! I don't know why I've never told you about it before! It's in Nashville, don't you like Nashville? You should totally go to this school in Nashville!" I was in shock. I took a step back laughing and said, "Okay so… I have to tell you something…"

I had no idea how much of a defining moment that was in my life. I had no idea how many times the story of that night would be told. I went home, researched the school, put my 30 days notice in on my apartment and began my transition. I didn't know anyone in Nashville, I barely knew anything about the school I had just applied to. All I knew was that I had this deep conviction in my heart that I needed to go. I had this urgency that I needed to go. There was something there that needed to be a part of my story, part of the next chapter. Doors in LA were closing, and little by little the doors in Nashville began to open.

There's been a lot about myself that I haven't always been a fan of, but I've gotta say I've always loved the part about me that just goes. Just applies, just moves, just talks, just starts, just goes.

The friend that told me about the school, Amy Pape, her story is one of the most beautiful stories that I've ever heard. Since this is my book and I get to say whatever I want, I just want to selfishly use this paragraph right here to tell you how amazing this woman is. I had met Amy Pape at Lauren's (another dear friend of mine) birthday party the September before, and we kept just ending up at the same birthday parties together. There were a lot of people at each party to hang out with, but each and every time I would find myself pulling Amy Pape to the side and asking her question after question and story after story. She was someone that I knew I was meant to know. Someone who I knew Jesus had a million reasons for me to know. Getting the opportunity to do so has been one of my favorite things in the whole world.

We kept meaning to get together because it is possible to chat over coffee just as much as it is in a cabin over birthday cake, but we kept having a hard time scheduling it. Since finding a time was so hard, we ended up planning a week or two in advance for an evening coffee hang. We made the date, and little did I know that those two weeks in between were going to be some of the most intense days I could possibly have. Those were the two weeks that I lost the majority of my friends. It's actually so crazy to think about this today looking back because the timing of my first coffee date with Amy Pape, who then became one the best friends I will ever have, couldn't have been more perfect. It's almost like God knew I was going to need a friend like her, so he had one waiting for me the whole time.

As soon as we sat down to chat, it was obvious that Amy Pape was going to become one of my favorite people in the whole world. I've never known someone that embodies the heart of Jesus the way that she does. I've never met someone who actually saw me, knew me, and loved me so intentionally the way that Amy Pape did. She's the kind of friend who will never fail to remind you who you are when you forget. Days of doubting myself and being weighed down by shame and fears are fixed within 5 minutes on a phone call with this girl. The term "love unconditionally" barely does her justice. I could go on forever and a day, but I just really want to make sure that whoever is reading this book knows how special that sweet, beautiful friend of mine is.

After just being kicked to the curb for sharing my story and who I was with the last group of friends, starting over with new people was a bit of a risk. It was risky but it was crucial if I ever wanted friends again and I knew it. Getting to know Amy and getting to be seen and loved anyway by her, which is the closest I've yet to experience to Jesus's love, was the most redemptive, healing thing in the world to come at this point in my life.

Someone told me recently after a being given a brief overview of my story that my life seems to be very "transitional." Well, that person was right. There actually might not be words that will give justice to the ridiculous amount of transitions and changes my life was headed for at this point. I ended up moving from my apartment to Alex's house for a month, then drove to Colorado and stayed at my parents house for another month, then off to Nashville to live in my first home for three months, then moved to a new home for three months, and as I sit in this cafe in Nashville, I'm preparing for another move to end off the year. Crazy, huh?

Obviously out of the strangely large amount of moves I took this year, the step from LA to Nashville was by far the most challenging. No, it wasn't because of the 30 hour drive, brand spanking new city to adjust to, or how expensive I later realized all of that was going to end up, but it was because I hadn't the slightest clue until that point how special LA had become to me. Yes, LA is dirty. Yes, LA is expensive, stressful, nearly impossible to find a decent parking spot anywhere without spending more money than you were about to on dinner. But LA was my home.

I would never be who I am without LA. I know what you're thinking, "No duh Jackie, everyone says things like that." But bear with me here for a minute. I was actually watching a video recently that I made talking about my first move to LA. I was bleach blonde, 19, and I was truly just stoked for whatever famous person I might run into on the street mainly so I could just go tell everyone about it. I wanted to go to Hollywood just for the sake of telling people that

I was in Hollywood. I was obsessed with cold pressed juice, organic-this or vegan-that, whatever the LA people were doing was what I wanted to be a part of. It was really just about the social media posts I was trying to make in an attempt to feel better about myself. The mindset that I had going into LA was probably the same as the majority of peoples' that were moving there as well, simply because that's just what LA is seen as. I didn't know why I was there, but I knew that there was purpose, even then. Whether that purpose was training dolphins or working in music, it didn't really matter yet as long as I was there.

I was 21 when I was getting ready to leave LA. I hated Hollywood, I only went to Beverly Hills for church (ironically), and I wouldn't drop nine dollars on kale juice if it was the last thing that I could buy (that changed, I'm pro-juice again, by the way, but at this time it was a hard "no"). And yet, my time in LA was so far from perfect and so close to messy, and every other word thesaurus.com can give me that means the same thing. It's a place that I got my heart broken, learned what love is, learned what grace means, let alone feels like, and how insanely hard it is to accept. It's the city that I learned what vulnerability actually means, and how scary it truly is to be. It's scary because you really never know what kind of response you're going to get. You never know whether the person really cares about your heart or just wants something to talk about to pass the time. How can you know for sure if you're truly going to be taken care of or not? But if we don't do it, if we continue to hide inside of our own heads and keep presenting this fake edited picture perfect version of what we want the world to see us as, everyone is just going to go around pretending that they're okay all the time and that's a pretty sad way to live, if you ask me.

LA taught me how absolutely terrifying it is to have a negative bank account balance while living in one of the most expensive cities in the country. It taught me how embarrassing that is, how vulnerable that is to talk about, and how to rely on Jesus to take care of me in the midst of it. Yes, I can tell you from personal experience that he does. Money is a hard topic and if we're not careful we end up depending on it for security, comfort, identity… and when you live in such an expensive city and can't afford to buy groceries and don't know if you're going to be able to pay rent, that's a scary place to be in. That being said, LA also taught me how to budget my money, and that drinking five large cups of coffee a day is not the smartest idea for my wallet, let alone my health and well being. I learned that I actually have no idea what I'm doing, and I don't think really anybody does if they're being honest with themselves. Life is hard. None of us are experts at it. I believe that we're all out here, or wherever you call home, doing the best that we know how, but none of us actually have this life figured out. My sister taught me that one of the best things you can say to someone that's going through a hard time is, "me too." There's power in knowing that it's okay to not always know what we're doing as long as we're doing it with people. That's the most important lesson out of all of this; how important people are and how terrible the idea of doing life alone actually is. The relationships that you build are what gets you through. Not your bank account, not your career, not even that extra-whip-Frappuccino, or whatever your classic Starbucks order is, but people. They're what feeds your soul and what you actually need to survive out there. Not just in LA, but anywhere really. Doing life alone is pointless, meaningless, and every word in between. That's why the first thing that God said was "not good" was for man to be alone. But it's not about who you're going to call to produce your next record, manage your text tour, or who you want to collab with next week. It's about who you're going to call at 2am when you feel like your life is falling apart and you need a shoulder to cry on, chocolate chip cookie dough, and just someone to tell you that everything is going to be okay. Yes, I do believe that I found myself in LA. But I also believe that if you take anyone out of their comfort zone and put them somewhere that they don't know, they'll find themselves too.

It wasn't until I was crying over a TV Ellen Degeneres gave me (a story for another time) that I realized how much my life was about to change. Sprawled out in the parking lot of a bank that I can't remember the name of, I was trying to figure out the best way to pack my last two years worth of memories into my little Toyota Avalon and leave enough room for my two best friends to make the road trip with me.

Everything hit me at once, right smack in the face. For some peculiar reason up until that moment, I had barely any fears about this move. I don't know if I was on some kind of false assumption that I was invincible, or on some kind of confidence high, but fear about moving wasn't real to me until then. I knew I didn't know anyone in Nashville, I knew I was about to say goodbye to my sister, my friends, my coffee shops, my apartment, my familiarity, my favorite grocery store, etc., but I felt fearless. The time couldn't have gone by fast enough, I thought, there were even times when I wanted to bail on all my plans and leave early in the middle of the night, without anyone knowing. That's how excited I was, and that's how ready I was to be done with California. But the second the LA memories began, the tears came along as well. I was pretty embarrassed to be honest, because crying in a random bank parking lot, holding a giant flat screen TV, doesn't make much sense when you don't know what's actually going on in my head. It can be quite confusing actually, and appear very spoiled "sweet sixteen birthday party gone wrong." Yet there I was, casually hiding behind a random car, hoping nobody would see me, finally starting to realize how much I actually loved LA. Yes, the traffic was terrible. Yes, the gas prices were straight up laughable. Yes, there were so many people who had hurt me, but, for some reason, saying goodbye became one of the hardest things I've ever had to do. I grew into myself in LA, and I had no idea what this next Nashville chapter in my life was going to look like. I was scared.

The roadtrip my friends and I took was an odd mix of breath-takingly incredible and obnoxiously emotional, with a side of funny. If anyone out there reading this has ever been in a car with their best friends for longer than 10 hours, you might be able to relate. This trip was by far the greatest road trip I've ever taken. I pulled up at about 5am to pick up Lauren and Amy Pape before we started the drive out to Nashville. Waiting in the car, sipping my heavily caffeinated espresso, I watched them run up to my car wearing matching red t-shirts with the words "Team JAX" on the back. Not too surprised because I already knew how amazing these friends of mine were, I just started to tear up. I had never felt that supported in something before. I'm not just talking about the t-shirts, these girls were truly just some of the most authentic, loyal, loving, incredible friends I could have ever asked for. This road trip was the most exciting, and yet the scariest thing I've ever done. It was just full of controversial feelings that didn't line up. But it was amazing, you know? We had the whole "stop wherever and whenever you feel like it" mentality, and we totally took full advantage of it.

My favorite part of the drive was when we pulled off on a random exit in Utah to grab a coffee, and, during casual conversation with the barista, we were informed that we were only two exits away from Zion National Park, which happened to be number one on Lauren's bucket list of National Parks she wanted to visit. By the way, I refer to Lauren as my professional adventurer friend. In a nutshell description; she's pretty much fully ready and prepared to go camping or on any other adventure at the drop of a hat at all times. So obviously we went to Zion. We spent the whole rest of the day there, actually.

It was literally a dream. There really is something about the beauty of nature that is unlike anything else in the world. There's something so special and indescribable that happens in my heart when I'm suddenly face to face with how small I actually am. It's that feeling you get when you're toes deep in the sand, taking in the unimaginable length and depth of the ocean. Or if you've ever been lucky enough to experience looking down into the Grand Canyon, or stand in the middle of a giant forest, with trees towering over everything you could see. That's how I felt as I stood up out of my sunroof as my friends drove me through the mountains of Zion; just small enough to realize that I'm living in a bigger story than I thought, and it might not be all about me after all.

For lack of better words, I felt like I was flying. Like this was a total Titanic moment, and I'm not ashamed to admit it. But what's really insane about all this nature stuff, what's really mind boggling about all of this as a whole is that the whole point of God creating nature was for us. The point of the beauty behind the forests and the flowers and the mountains, was all for us. Imagine the most beautiful waterfall, mountain range, sunset, etc., and try to understand as fully as you can that it was created purely for you. What's the reason? Love. Love is the reason, it always is. God is a creative God, and he loves us so well in that. It's all part of him wooing us, romancing us, all that girly stuff that is weirdly hard for me to write in this book, but it's the truth. That's one reason why it bothers me so much when people say there's no more miracles, or that there's not proof that God exists. Look outside, there's your miracle. Look at the mountain ranges or the sunsets. Look at the leaves changing in the fall or the flowers growing in the spring. There's your miracle. But my favorite part about all of this nature and sunset talk is this; God created the mountains, the trees, the flowers, the sunsets, the oceans, and everything else under the sun. But out of everything, out of the most beautiful scenes that artists make millions to paint, or cost people thousands to own, God still chose us. Out of all of that, we are what God loves the most. We are what is most beautiful to the one who created all of that. Why? I honestly can't tell you. Other than the peculiar fact that we're somehow made in his image, that really doesn't make sense to me. But if I'm being honest with you, sometimes on a bad day I'll look at a picture of a sunset and remember this fact, and I start to feel a little bit better about myself. Which, I think, is one of God's intentions for making the sunsets so beautiful.

Jesus

"If the Gospel of Jesus is relational, that is, if our brokenness
will be fixed not by our understanding of theology but
by God telling us who we are, then this would require
a kind of intimacy of which only heaven knows."

– Donald Miller

I REALIZE THAT THIS MIGHT BE AN UNUSUAL
time in my story to ask, but is anyone confused here? Is anyone wondering how I went from getting blackout-drunk on the regular to talking about the love and beauty of God? What could have happened to make a change this sudden take place in my life creating that kind of shift? Well, thank you for asking, if you did, because that right there is my favorite story of all to tell.

Growing up, I guess I can get away with saying that I was raised as a Christian. I have all the memories of going to Sunday School, watching Veggie Tales and singing every single "Silly Songs with Larry" jingle that I could keep up with, having the occasional Bible study with my family as a kid, and even collecting more badges on my Awana vest than I could find a spot to sew on. But to be honest with you, I never had a clue what any of that meant. I went through the motions because I thought it was just a part of life. My parents said it was important, so I listened. Deciding that I was a Christian felt no different than deciding that I would go to school on Monday. I remember my dad telling me over and over again that I needed to get baptised, but nothing inside of me wanted to do that for any reason other than to get my dad to stop nagging me. Sorry Dad, just trying to be real here. It didn't make sense and I had no interest in actually being a part of it for anything more than an hour one sunday every other month when I had to. I did what I had to do to get by, but at the end of the day I didn't know who Jesus was and I just wanted to continue doing whatever I wanted to do, simply because I could. I didn't want to get involved in something that was about to tell me to stop living my life the way I wanted to live it. I didn't want to submit to something that didn't even make sense to me in the first place, yet seemed full of people telling me what I can and cannot do. Besides, the people that were part of it seemed boring to me. Just being honest here. I really enjoyed drinking and smoking weed, and I was told that the Bible suggests against that and I didn't think that sounded like very much fun.

As I've mentioned a few of times already, the year that I genuinely believe I was in my darkest, most painfully lost place was in 2014 when I went on my first tour. It was the year I went on that tour after moving in with my sister in LA and her boyfriend hired me to be his assistant. This was the climax year of parties, mistakes, boy problems and shame, but it was also the year that a seed was planted. It's funny how that works, you know? Sometimes the raddest things come from the messiest things. Just ironic. It's kind of like that whole "purpose in the pain" type of thing, but in a much cooler and much less cliche kind of way. You feel me?

There was this girl on the tour that was doing life with me at the time, and there was, without a doubt, something extremely different about her. When I say "doing life with," I mean living life in the closest way humanly possible. I don't know if any of you have ever lived on a bus, but when you do, you tend to get to know the other people living on the bus on a pretty specifically intimate way that is unlike anything else. This is like a shoulder-to-shoulder, no-possible-way-of-hiding-when-you-have-to-go-poop sort of lifestyle. Everyone is going to know everyone's business, bladder size, morning breath scent, and midnight snacking choices.

Picture it like this: young, very blonde, 19-year-old Rebel Jackie hopping off her first out of country airplane into Vancouver, slightly nervous but not willing to show it, stumbling onto a tour bus full of mainly dudes and not one bit of familiarity in sight. I threw my embarrassingly oversized red suitcase on the best bunk I could find, grabbed a quick glance at myself in the mirror, and headed out for what I thought was about to be the coolest experience of my life. This was a time that I almost got the word "wanderlust" tattooed on my wrist, by the way, if that paints any clearer of a picture for you about what I was looking for.

Then suddenly, there she was. There was the girl that was about to impact my life in more ways than I would have believed if someone would have told me back then. Nervous yet excited herself, she walked onto the bus with a big cheery grin across her face. Reaching out to shake her hand, it was almost as if I could sense the pureness in her heart she carried that very instant. I didn't know why, but all of a sudden I just wanted to know everything there was to know about her. I wanted to ask her every question I could pull out of my brain because there was something about her story that I felt like I needed, I just didn't know what it was.

The truth is, in my whole life I had never seen such pure, unconditional love come from someone and I didn't know what it was or how to accept it. She saw exactly what I was doing. She saw the choices that I was making and the kind of life that I was living, but for some reason it didn't matter to her. The many mornings that I would wake up miserably hungover and angry, she'd be the one bringing me Advil and loving me, checking in to see if my heart was okay. I didn't understand why. She was up the night before as well, she saw me take shot after shot, she saw me pass out on the ground, wrapped up in a blanket, outside the bus. At least I thought she did, anyway. If not, this part might be a little awkward when she reads it. My point is, this is someone who saw my life and chose love over judgment. It's not even that she chose to love me, it's that I don't think she could really help it. She didn't see me and try to tell me what to do or attempt to fix me, she saw me and just tried to be my friend.

"What is wrong with this girl?" I would constantly think to myself. "Does she know something I don't?" I knew I didn't deserve her care and it made me uncomfortable. The more love she would show me, the more guilty I would feel for the way I was living; the more undeserving I knew for a fact I must be. But there was something different about this girl, something she had that I wanted. What was I missing in my heart that she had in hers that made her love people the way that she did? Can you imagine waking up in just shame and self hatred and there's this girl that is just loving you anyway? The more love I would feel, the more broken I knew that I was.

The Bible says that when someone really loves Jesus, Jesus lives in them. It says that when someone has Jesus in them, they start to be able to love people the way that Jesus does, and it's unlike anything else in the world. That being said, this was my first experience of getting to know Jesus. I had nothing to compare it to because, for my whole life, the only "knowing Jesus" that I knew, the only Christian religion that I had ever been around was just not that. It was rules, judgment, people saying, "I don't do this because I'm a Christian," or people quoting Scripture to me when I was having a hard time, throwing in a "bless your heart" at the end to make it sound pretty. None of that made sense, nor was it appealing to me because I didn't see the change in people's lives that the Bible was claiming to make. I never felt good enough for it so I hid from it instead. Never did someone just simply love me as authentically and purely as this girl did on this tour bus when I needed it more than I ever would. That's what changes lives. That was the start of my journey and what made me realize that there might just be something more to this Christianity stuff after all.

After that seed was planted in my heart on tour, something shifted. I was sitting in the green room upstairs at the last show, at the last venue, in the last city of my first tour. Other band members would make their way in and out to snack on the free chips and Red Bull we got for being a band, or to grab a guitar string or some other musical thing they forgot. I smiled at them, and stared, for the first time in a very long time, at a blank word document on my computer. This felt scary to me. It felt too honest, and seeing as I had never used or heard of the word vulnerable before, it wasn't something I was familiar with. But I stared at that blank page because something inside of me told me that something was wrong and writing it out, the real stuff out, might help a little. That's when I started journaling. I sat in that green room and wrote out all my fears, why I thought they were there, and what I thought I even wanted. Right there in Buffalo, New York of all places, I realized that I just wanted to be loved.

I really did just feel dirty. I felt so distant from who I knew I was meant to be. I felt tired and lonely, and I really wasn't too fond of it. The thing is, I wasn't any further broken at the end of the tour than at the beginning, but there was a new awareness of it that I wasn't used to sitting with. It kind of felt like someone was holding up a mirror for me to see my life and the choices I was making, and I couldn't even close my eyes to escape the view.

That night I sat in my boss Steve's hotel room, and for the first time we had a real conversation about what was going on. It wasn't even about the mistakes we made really, it was mostly just a talk about what was going on in my head and my heart, and why I felt the way that I did. I had never had a real conversation like that before. I had never shared something so vulnerable before with another human being.

I woke up late and missed my flight, so I ended up stranded at the Buffalo, NY airport for about ten hours. I know that wasn't actually the end of the world, but it definitely felt like it at the time. Let's face it, happy or sad, ten hours at any airport is never a walk in the park. Unless of course you have some sort of passion for over priced bananas and angry security guards, which I definitely do not. I'm talking like $1.50 for one lousy banana, and it didn't even come with peanut butter! All I did in that airport was think for ten hours straight. I would think, write, read, and cry a little bit. But something was happening.

I landed in LA, set up camp on the couch that would be my home again for the next few months, and, as usual attempted to drown out my thoughts with a TV show next to my friend Epps and a bowl of cereal. After the first day there, I was given a book that was about to play a major role in what was about to happen to me. Books seem to change my life a lot, but this one was definitely the first one to do so at this point in time. I was given the book *The Gifts of Imperfection* by Brene Brown, and I popped it open just because I felt like I should, and I read. After the first day, reading turned into a new routine. If you ask my friend and roommate at the time, Eppic, he'll most likely tell you that a day of mine involved waking up, working out, and reading my book for a few hours before I turned on *How I Met Your Mother*, or some show like that. That, plus a few apples and peanut butter, you had the simple life of Jackie G. The cool thing about when I read that book was that it happened right after the walls were down far enough for me to see that I was messed up. After what had just happened on tour with Steve, it was plain as day to me that my life was broken. I had pieces of my heart that I was terribly ashamed of, and this book was the first thing to tell me that I was still okay. This book was the first time I ever heard of the word "vulnerability," learned what shame actually was, and that I'm definitely not the only person in the world who feels it. But the thing is, shame or no shame, mistakes or no mistakes, I was still loved and worthy *exactly where I was*. I had never heard that before. "Here's what is truly at the heart of wholeheartedness: Worthy now, not if, not when, we're worthy of love and belonging now. Right this minute. As is." That was absolutely new information to me. It was relieving, yet hard to believe. More than new information actually, it was a new way of life. A new perspective on who I was and what I actually needed. It was the first time I really, truly believed that I wasn't alone. It was the first thing to tell me that even with my flaws and mistakes, I was still loveable. Without something telling me that, whether I had any business hearing it or not, I would have never been able to accept what came next.

The day was October 29th, 2014. I was back home in Colorado after spending some more time in LA after tour. The time in LA was spent reading books, writing in journals, and trying to do life with my sister and her new friends for a while. I was home now though, home and back to the same gut feeling of loneliness I had felt before and I didn't want to tell a single soul. I laid on my couch in my parent's living room all day, everyday, not doing anything but watching Gilmore Girls in silence. No laughing, no emotions, just blank stares while Rory Gilmore drank another cup of coffee and made clever banter with her mom all day. Literally all day. That show was hilarious.

That morning, I got a phone call from Steve. Steve had gone back to LA for a little while. I wasn't the only one feeling shame from what we done and the choices we were making. He was on his own quest to figure out his life as well. It felt like we were both at the end of ourselves, and he went away to a men's retreat in the mountains to see what was going on. I don't like to claim that a lot of things were specially orchestrated by God because I've seen a lot of people overdo that to the max and it just takes the sacredness out of the true moments it happens, but this was, *without a doubt*, one of those moments.

"What does God mean to you?" he asked.

I know I built this moment up, and you're probably reading this expecting tears and worship right now, but I was honestly appalled that he would ask such a thing. Like, come on man, that's a big question! How could someone ask me something like that? Of course I knew who God was! "God created the world," I thought to myself. That was as far as I got. I really did know he was real, but other than that I didn't have a clue.

I got off the phone with him that morning and was just angry. I really don't know how to explain why, so I guess maybe I was just embarrassed. Either way, I was determined to find an answer for him. I knew who God was! I had to prove myself. So I went outside to my backyard and I opened this app on my phone that Steve had downloaded for me while we were on tour. I don't really remember why he did that, but I didn't find a reason to pull it up until now. I turned on a sermon by this guy Matt Chandler. I had never heard of him, but his name seemed promising for some reason. He sounded a little angry, but I kind of liked it. I laid on the grass and listened for a bit until the next thing I knew, I was on my fourth sermon. What the heck? What was happening? I was confused so I went up to my room and I found this old Bible that I hadn't touched in years. I opened it up and the bookmark was placed on the very first page of 1 Corinthians. Today it's my favorite book in the Bible, but at the time I had never even heard of a Corinthian. I had no idea what it was, but I just started reading. I got through the first chapter about how the wisdom of the world is foolish to God, and how the wisdom of God is foolish to the world. I read about how God uses foolish things to actually shame the ones who think they're wise. That's when things started to click. I got on my knees and I prayed. I felt like an idiot. I had no idea what I was supposed to say, all I knew was that something remarkable was happening in my heart and I didn't want to mess it up.

> "The message of the cross is foolish to those who are headed for destruction! But we who are being saved know it is the very power of God. As the Scriptures say, 'I will destroy the wisdom of the wise and discard the intelligence of the intelligent.' So where does this leave the philosophers, the scholars, and the world's brilliant debaters? God has made the wisdom of this world look foolish. Since God in his wisdom saw to it that the world would never know him through human wisdom, he has used our foolish preaching to save those who believe."
>
> – 1 Corinthians 1:18-20

That right there, that's what got me. All of a sudden everything made sense. This world is backwards, it's twisted and we're all being fooled by our own selves and selfish desires. We're being fooled into thinking that we want one thing. We think we want a big house or a fancy car, or the best career or spouse to make us happy. We think we have to be the smartest or the funniest, or the best at sports to be okay. We think that's what we need. But God is bigger than that, smarter than that, and better than that, and I was now newly convicted of this truth. I was living all wrong and I was now coming face to face with myself and all of my flaws, mistakes, confusions... all of it. What happened that night was that I now had the truth in my heart that God loved me right where I was at, was pursuing me, and had so much better for me than I could have ever imagined. I was chasing the wrong things. My desire was actually to be known and loved and accepted, but I was going after it all wrong. That right there was the start of my relationship with Jesus. That was when I learned that the Bible wasn't just a big book of rules and stories that we were "supposed" to read. It wasn't just a book of verses to be memorised for a patch on our Christianity sashes. I learned that hiding from God was not only impossible, but didn't make any sense. I learned that drinking and partying with my friends was, as cliche as this sounds, not the answer to feeling loved or being cool. It was never going to fulfill me the way that I thought it would, and now I had to face that. I really didn't know a lot, but what I did know was that if this Jesus guy was real, I wanted to know everything there was to know about him.

It had been about two years since I was living on that tour bus until I got to see my sweet friend from the road again, the friend that was my light in the darkness. Within those two years, my life had been rocked a bit, for lack of better words. Two long, exhausting, pushing, jaw-dropping years. Then one day, there was her name on my phone, followed by a message telling me she was in Nashville and wanted to get lunch. Way too many emotions to list were all being felt in my heart. I was nervous, I was excited, and I was relieved. I knew I had to tell her the truth. I had to tell her what was really going on in my heart on that tour, the mistakes I was trying to cover up and the shame I was trapped under. I wanted her to know that, but more than anything else in the world I just wanted her to know how much she changed my life. It's not everyday that we get the opportunity to share that with people who change our lives. It's an interesting thing to hear, I'm sure.

I sat anxiously at Edgehill Café, pretending to look over the menu of egg scrambles and espresso options while I waited for her to walk in. This was a day that I wasn't sure would ever happen, but was so thankful for, it's insane. Hair pulled back in the cutest pig tail braids I had ever seen, Lizzie walked in.

"LIZZIE!"

"JACKIE!"

"You look so cute, look at you!" I screamed

"Awwww Jackie, YOU look so cute!"

We went on like that for a good five minutes or so, like any girls do after they haven't seen each other in a while. From then came five minutes of small talk, mainly about the egg choices and reminiscing banter about how we used to live off of bananas and a shared jar of peanut butter in the old tour days. But then came the time, I shared with my friend the real story about who I was, and what I had been going through. The funny thing is, out stories were a lot more similar than I expected. Tears were shed, of course, hugs were given generously, and I had my friend back in the newest, most beautiful way possible.

I love that story. I love it because I believe that it's proof that Jesus had my back the whole time. It shows that even though I didn't know it was him, he still so desperately wanted to show me that pure, life-altering love at such a dark point in my life. A time in my life when I was living in every other way than the he would have wanted.

As Christians, I believe we tend to get a little too caught up in thinking that we've got to go around and teach everyone about Jesus and make sure people know the rules and aren't sinning, or at least the really big and bad obvious kinds of sinning. The kinds of sinning like drinking or saying too many curse words. We stress ourselves out trying to prove to people that we're living a clean, pure life because we're Christians and we're good. We think that if we can represent ourselves as spotless to the outside world, and we tell them all the rules and all the facts then we'll get them converted into our cool Christian club. None of that came close to saving me. People pretending to have their lives in order, pretending not to have any problems or struggles or real pain in their lives did nothing but push me away. None of that planted the seed in my heart that made me actually ask myself the big questions. What was I missing? The kind of love that my friend was embodying. That's what changed everything.

We have got to stop going around throwing Bible verses in people's faces and telling them that they're wrong. Handing someone a list of do's and don'ts is not going to speak to their heart. It might change them for a week or a month, maybe even a year. I mean, it worked on me for a little while at different times in my life at least, but if you're not getting to the real core of who they actually are and who Jesus is meant to be for them, it just doesn't make much sense. If you're not giving them an actual purpose to change, which is only found in love itself, then you're not going to do anything but sound like a big, loud, annoying cymbal, and nobody actually enjoys those things anyway. None of that changed me. It's love that changed me. Love is what makes someone look at you and see something different in your eyes. The only way we're ever going to make an impact in this world is if we throw off our pride and just love people where they're at and for who they are. That's not easy. Trust me, I'm fully aware of that. Sometimes loving people where they're at, broken and angry and sometimes just plain cruel can be hard. But when we do, we get that much closer to discovering the true heart of who Jesus actually is. That's freedom.

~~~~~

Believe it or not, meeting Jesus that night in October did not solve all of my problems. As much as I would have loved it to, I was still human, just like the rest of the world, and still faced what seemed like every insecurity in the book. I find it interesting actually how some people see Christians and assume that, since they're a Christian, they have their life all together. Or they think after they become a Christian their life will all magically fall into place like a storybook fairytale. I think that's what keeps a lot of people away from it, actually. It's what makes people think that they're not good enough yet. They think that before they can go to church, they have to "clean up their act." Nope, not the truth. Not at all. As sad and ironic as it sounds, coming to terms with my own brokenness and desperate need for something bigger than me did not magically turn me into a perfect human.

I ended up moving back to LA in January of 2015, shortly after all this happened. I had originally wanted to move to Nashville at this time but felt pretty torn, so when I would ask around, people would tell me that, "God is not a God of confusion; He's a God of peace." Okay… not sure what that meant exactly but I did know that thinking about Nashville I felt uncertain, and thinking about LA I felt peace. So I packed up my 2002 Toyota Avalon and headed west for the third time.

Over the next six months I practically turned into the biggest Bible nerd of my time. All I wanted to do was read my Bible, talk about Jesus, and listen to sermons all day everyday. It got to be so much that I was starting to get told to, "cool it with the Jesus stuff. You don't want to get burnt out." But those words weren't going to stop me. I read book after book, Bible story after Bible story... you name it and I would read it. I walked to the same Starbucks down the street almost every single day to drink my extra large piping hot Americano and read my Bible. My old friends probably thought I was crazy, especially the ones who knew my life from before. I had no idea how to talk about it with them so I just didn't.

I had continued working for Steve for the first half of the year. I was attached to him, and had a major fear of leaving the only job that I felt capable of doing, especially in a city like LA. However oddly enough, things were different between us this time around. It was weird, but the more passionate I became about Jesus, the more passionate Steve would become. There was an aspect of hope, an aspect of truth that was evident in this new chapter. Steve quit drinking,

73

and I joined him. It was interesting because the man who I made the greatest mistakes with, I was now growing the most with. If redemption comes from Jesus, then Jesus was all over that.

Before all this Jesus stuff happened, I had never been part of a church before. I was at a point in my life where I had to make a decision; either I believed all this Bible stuff or I didn't, and I wanted to believe it. So I decided to do what it said and join a church. We went church hopping like crazy, but the one that caught my attention week after week was called City Church in Beverly Hills. This church was crazy cool. This guy Judah Smith flies from Seattle to LA every week to preach to our campus out of different hotel ballrooms. It started as a Bible study, but now became the home of some of the best people I've ever met.

Since none of the guys wanted to commit and make a decision on the church they wanted to call home, I decided to make my own decision and attend the City. I put down Steve's email for a community group, seeing as though I had never experienced real community before, and we started a group that grew to about thirty people crammed inside a tiny LA apartment. I'm not sure why I put Steve's email instead of mine. I was probably just scared.

This community group became one of the most special things that I had ever been a part of. Week after week old and new faces would show, and we would just sit around and talk about Jesus for hours. But it wasn't just that, these people actually became some of my closest friends at the time. We did life together, had each others backs, and that is what church is meant to be. If I learned anything from this experience, it's that church is meant to be exactly that, community. After group late at night, we would all walk to IHOP, where, no joke, I would bring a cup full of cereal to eat so I wouldn't have to spend money while we were there, and just continue to do life together. We played this game called "What Are the Odds?" which, one night, made me have to down a spoonful of what was most likely the world's spiciest hot sauce, burning everything inside of me. It also got my friend Chad having to stand up and yell, "YOU get a free pancake, and YOU get a free pancake, YOU ALL GET FREE PANCAKES!" before we left. That was awesome.

However amongst all this growth and community and fun times, I was still attached to Steve, still felt utterly ashamed from the mistakes we had made, and he was still my sister's ex-boyfriend. I didn't want to face that. I wanted to live where I was in my new community and new life, but I didn't want to do the work of dealing with my past. In order to avoid, my coping mechanism was turning off my emotions. What's funny is that I don't think I actually realized this until right now as I'm writing this paragraph. I was so consumed by the shame of what had happened with my boss, and so deep in denial that I was wrong, that to cope with myself and my shame, I had to shut down my emotions to avoid feeling that. Interestingly enough, it's actually part of how our bodies are created as a coping mechanism that is meant to protect the heart from trauma. But the scary thing about shutting down the emotions to avoid feeling shame was that I ended up shutting down my emotions to feel much of anything. Moment by moment, I started to become somewhat of a shell. I was uncomfortable with crying, with feelings, and with anything close to negativity. I was scared of it because I just didn't want to face it.

It got so bad that when my friends and I went to see the movie *Inside Out*, I was the only one who didn't cry. That's an insanely great movie, people! Come on now. If nothing else makes you believe it, this shows that I clearly had a problem.

All of this shame left me asking my friend Abbie one day a really important question. It was a simple, yet life altering question for me.

"Hey so… I know that God loves us. I get that. But I really don't understand why." I asked Abbie that question purely because I still didn't think that someone who was as broken as me could be loved, especially by someone as perfect as God.

"He loves you because you're his daughter, Jackie." Abbie answered me without even having to think twice. Abbie was my first new friend in LA. I went to that girl for almost every question in the book. You're the best, Abbie.

That moment in the car after she answered that question was the beginning of a whole new kind of relationship with Jesus. I had no idea. Whether I would admit it or not, I knew that my life was messy. I knew that I had made some of the worst mistakes of my life, and I desperately wanted to avoid dealing with them. But because of those mistakes, it made absolutely no sense why this perfect creator of the world wanted me. Of all people, why me? I think the reason I was so avoidant of my feelings was because deep down I knew the truth of my mistakes, and I knew that if I entertained my real feelings long enough then I would have to act on them. So instead of dealing with it, I just kept my head up and ignored it. I spent my time studying the Bible, talking about Jesus, and hanging out with friends as much as possible. I was hiding.

———

I was sitting next to my friend Caroline (who, by the way, is the trendiest and cutest little human I've ever met), when I got an email that changed my life. We were driving back from my other friend Lauren's (the professional adventurer) camping birthday party. Caroline and I were in the middle of conversation most likely about how much she loves the band The 1975 or how we were really thankful we didn't get stuck in quicksand like everyone else did that day and lose our sandals, when I looked down at my phone and saw an email saying that I was accepted into this ministry group called Christ Life that I was on a waiting list for. I didn't know too much about the group, all I knew was that my friend Abbie had raved about it and told me how it apparently changed her life and she thinks that everyone should do it. A lot of things can change someone's life, but Abbie never really let me down when it came to recommendations of things and such so I took her word for it and looked into the thing. Abbie was a wise friend. She was really funny because she either dressed super girly, or super ghetto. There wasn't much of an in-between. Anyway, the group was an hour away, and it started the very next day. I was in.

Christ Life was a group that met once a week to go through the different phases of our lives and deal with our *stuff*. We went through each time period, ages 0-2, 2-5, 5-8, etc., and wrote these letters to our current selves from our younger selves in those ages. The point was to process through our lives and find out what events happened that lead us to believe these different lies about ourselves that we've been stuck with. We would pull out the lies, discuss the emotions that they developed, and then worked together to learn the truths about who we actually are as children of God.

I pulled up to the house, nervous as an intense introvert on the first day at a new school, and sat in my car. It's not that I was trying to be fashionably late or anything, I just couldn't get myself to go in. It was one of those moments where I didn't really know why I was so scared, but my body wouldn't budge. So I sat, stared, texted all my friends for some moral support, and sat some more. After building up my courage as much as I could, I choked back my fears and walked up to the front door. Feeling as confident as one could wearing a new Target cardigan, I pulled myself together and knocked. I felt so awkward, it's not even funny. After being greeted by a lady who could easily rank in the top five of the World's Kindest Humans, things started to lighten up a bit. I sat down on the couch and introduced myself to the four other women, all almost twice my age, and twiddled my thumbs for a bit while we waited to start. If I had known how much I was about to pour out of my heart to these ladies, if I had any idea how impactful the room I was sitting in was about to be, odds are I wouldn't of believed it.

One of the biggest obstacles that I came face to face with in that group was that I continued to effortlessly put a smile over my face and pretend like everything was okay in hopes of avoiding dealing with my problems. I don't know where I learned to do that, but there was no possible way this group of women was going to let me continue to do so. They saw me, broken pieces and all, and they were so determined to love me and work with me through the pain that a fake smile could never actually fix. This group taught me that my emotions are okay. My emotions are what makes me human and allow me to love people and relate to them. Emotions are what connect us to each other, so without them, what's the point? I learned that God is an extremely emotional God, and he created us to be the same way on purpose. He's not just emotional, he's poetic, sensitive, and really does love us a lot. It doesn't make sense how he does it, but he does. Crying in baseball might not be okay, but in other places it might not be so bad after all.

This group of women were literally a group of warriors. A group of warriors, and a group of mothers. Since day one with them we were sharing things that sometimes we've never even said out loud before. There were things that I shared with them while we were still complete and utter strangers, that I had never even thought about before. Like come on here, imagine writing yourself a letter, being as vulnerable WITH YOURSELF as possible about what you're feeling and experiencing during the most traumatic memories you can think of, then having to read that letter out loud to four women who you just met the week before. It was scary, but weirdly felt so safe. Crazy safe, actually. I think there was something deep in my heart that knew that these women cared about me, and when someone really cares about you it's always easier to let the guards down. I don't know if that's a safe and great thing for just anybody anywhere, but the specific women that I was with made it to be one of the most healing things I've ever done.

It took me until the second to last week of reading letters at group until it finally happened; there were the tears. I was embarrassed, but weirdly relieved at the same time. I sat there on the couch and just let it all out. Everybody tried handing me kleenex and wanted to hug me at the same time. It wasn't even the story about the rape that got me, it was the stuff about where I was currently at with my sister and my boss and just, it hit me hard I guess. Until that moment, I actually thought I was turning into a robot. I never thought I would be so excited to cry in my life.

Once I was able to come in touch with my emotions, I started to feel again. I started to feel loved, validated, accepted, you name it. I felt all the feels. I felt the pure joys in life, but also the deep sorrows. I was suddenly able to connect and empathise with people on this whole new level that truly felt foreign to me before. I learned that it's okay to not be okay, and being vulnerable about where you're actually at is the kindest thing you can do for not only yourself, but for those around you. It actually has the power to create the safest space for others to do the same thing. I also learned that everyone has a story. Everyone has a reason for why they are the way that they are. There's a reason behind the insecurities, reason behind the mistakes, and reason behind the smile.

I had it all wrong before, really. I was under the impression, for lots of different reasons, that emotions turn people away. I built it up in my head somehow that crying is annoying and nobody would want to be around me if I were any more emotional of a person than I was leading on. The idea that people only wanted to be around me if I was the "happy go lucky" sweet little Jackie just grew deeper and deeper as truth to me, so retraining my brain for the opposite took some work.

Even my YouTube videos started to change. They went from being written out and rehearsed simple Bible lessons with a bunch of scriptures, to me turning on my camera, not having any idea how or what I was going to say, then somehow ending up sharing the most vulnerable parts of my heart with complete strangers on the internet. I even ended up crying on camera once which was huge to say the least.

But out of all of these things, my relationship with God is what changed the most. Suddenly I felt the freedom to get honest. So honest that it scared me. It's funny because reading through my journal of that year, I go from regularly writing down Bible verses and explaining what I was learning about Paul or Peter, to expressing my deepest fears and anxieties, loves and dreams, all of that gushy stuff that I wouldn't dare tap into before. I opened myself up to be known. I felt insane. I annoyed myself at times, but oh my friend it was so good. It just felt like, for a moment, God didn't want me to get to whatever level of Bible knowledge I was trying to get to. He didn't want me to focus on leading a Bible study or beating LA traffic to get to church early enough to help get the coffee ready, he just wanted me. He wanted my heart. Raw, broken, imperfect, and real. And I was finally at a place where I was able to give it to him.

I started to hear God's voice more clearly than I ever thought was possible, which made our relationship really fun. Hearing his voice became this whole new world to me, a new world of having a relationship with a Father who knew me and loved me anyway. But as fun as it was, it meant that I really did have to deal with my stuff. Now that I was more aware of what was going on in my heart, ignoring it wasn't an option anymore. So, in order to continue to experience the genuine love that came from this new way of life, I had to deal with my *stuff*.

As much as I wished I had finally arrived after all this, being in touch with my emotions never meant that I was now "perfect." Perfection was not, and will never be, the point. God called David a man after his own heart. He claims he doesn't pick favorites, but if he did I think it's obvious that David would take that role. But what made David so special? Obviously he was nowhere close to perfect, he was just honest. Psalms is by far the most emotional book in the Bible, yet also the messiest. David goes back and forth from praising God and thrilled about life to wanting to crush babies heads on rocks. I'm not making that up, I promise. I think the reason God called David a man after his own heart was because no matter how low it got for him, he never pretended to have it all together. He was as honest as ever in how he felt when he was talking to God. He told God exactly how he felt, baby head crushing and all. That was the beauty of it. He gave God all of him, and still held so tightly onto the truth of how much God loved him through it all as well. No matter how low it got, God was still good and David still knew it. Look through any of the psalms and you'll find that even the most distressed chapters end with him talking about the goodness of God. He faced himself, but he still knew the truth. I believe that is what separated him from the rest. That's how I want to live my life, vulnerable and honest so much it hurts, but always holding onto what's true. What's true is that God loves me, God is good, and I am set free.

Tension

"I can no more understand the totality of God than the pancake I made for breakfast this morning understands the complexity of me."

– Donald Miller

HAVE YOU EVER BEEN IN A ROOM FULL OF PEOple that all think one thing and you think the other? Not just in a slight disagreement type of way, but I'm talking passion and heartfelt belief for a certain way of life, and you feel differently without a clear vision on why? Well long story very short, I have.

Remember that ministry school I was talking about earlier? The one I decided to move across the country for? Yep, that one. Well you see the thing is, I ended up dropping out. To be honest with you, I was on the fence about staying in the school since before it even began. You see, before I moved to Nashville, I had one major church experience. I was involved in my church in LA that I absolutely loved, and I'm not sure what it would be classified as other than non-denominational. I could be wrong, but that's what I would call it if it were up to me. Only knowing Jesus for about 2 years, I tended to take what all my Christian friends told me as truth most of the time. I thought that if someone prayed really well and said the right spiritual things, they must be right and I should learn from them because I'm young and a "new Christian." That was my mindset, and after being pretty badly stabbed in the back by some of those Christian friends right before I moved to Nashville, I figured I needed a new method of learning who to trust and what not. That being said, my biggest prayer for life in my new home was that I would have discernment. Oddly enough, Jesus decided to answer that prayer. Funny how he does that. However, having this new discernment was a little bit confusing for me at first. I found myself questioning people, seeing through the fake smiles, fake attitudes, and fake niceness that I was never able to see through before. It gave me this new sense of power to choose what kind of people I wanted to have in my life, but it didn't always feel very good. It was confusing because now that I had this authority of knowing and choosing who was going to be in my life, I then had to learn how to trust my own decisions. I needed to learn to trust this discernment that Jesus gave me, which is a lot harder than it sounds. I genuinely wish I could just go with the flow and agree with everyone and have everyone be my best friend, but it's just not reality.

Anyway, my discernement got decently broken in at the beginning of the school. Before I moved to Nashville, I couldn't have been more excited to start. It was all I wanted to talk about and I spent hours on end watching testimony videos, reading blogs, and just dreaming about what my experience was going to be like. My heart was open to receive any and everything they wanted to teach me, which I thought was exactly where I needed to be. However, a week or so before my long awaited first day of school, something happened that completely threw me off. I was at a birthday party with a good amount of people that I didn't know, some were a part of my school and some weren't, and it turned into a worship night that got, well, different. Don't get me wrong, worship is one of my favorite things in the world and I'm by no means against the Holy Spirit, but at this party I ended up being overwhelmingly pressured to speak in tongues, and surrounded by a lot of uncomfortable things that I haven't ever experienced before. I'm not sure where you stand with that, and for all I know this chapter might make you a little mad or a little uncomfortable, but either way I want it share it with you because I believe that it matters.

I ended up walking out on the worship night, ran up to the parking lot of the apartment complex, plopped myself down on the curb and cried. I wasn't really sure why, but I knew that there was something in my heart that didn't feel right being there. Luckily there were a couple really good friends of mine who witnessed this whole thing go down that came to see if I was okay, and one of the first things they told me was that I shouldn't go to that school. That was absolutely terrifying for me to hear from them. I mean I moved across the country for this school, I had been so excited and invested so much! These two friends of mine really cared about me though, and really loved Jesus, so why did they so strongly disagree with these other people that really loved Jesus? Aren't we all trying to do the same thing? It was confusing and I had never felt such a strong divide in the Christian community before, so I ended up calling my sister and her best friend to tell them what happened. Instantly after hearing my experience, they both told me not to do the school as well.

"Don't do that school, Jackie. It's bad news."

Shortly after this birthday party, I had to go to a church conference that I signed up to volunteer for. After what happened at the party, not one little piece of me wanted to go be around this kind of environment again. It was an extremely hyped up conference and there were some big names speaking there that I had never heard of, but were very loved by that circle of church folk. On the last night of the conference it was the last session of worship that left me running out, getting in my car, and ugly crying the whole way home. I'm probably making myself sound like an emotional mess and who knows, I just might be. But the experience at this conference left me even more confused and upset than the birthday party did. Without going into too much detail, there was simply a whole lot of loud spiritual things going on that were actually terrifying. So yeah, it was pretty intense and, due to the fact that it was claiming to be about my Jesus, it made me really upset.

I really didn't have many words or explanations as to why, but this honestly started one of the most confusing, frustrating times of my faith that I had ever experienced. I started doubting everything I thought I knew. I doubted my ability to hear God, I doubted God's ability to speak to me, and I just doubted God in general. I'm not trying to be dramatic, I just felt absolutely helpless. Being in an environment of worship that made me feel as scared, violated, and uncomfortable as it did, I felt like something special and sacred was stolen from me. Maybe you know what I mean, or maybe you don't, but my relationship with Jesus just flat out felt invaded.

I was confused because, if all this "weird stuff" was true, I just wanted to know it and believe it for myself. But if it wasn't true, then why were all these trusted big name Christians and leaders that were all about it? Why did something that is supposedly from Jesus make me feel that scared and confused? Nothing about it made sense. If it was all these big Christian leaders versus me, there was no possible way that I thought I could have been right. I mean, I was barely going on two years of being a Christian and these people were leading churches! All I knew was that, as cliche as it sounds, my faith was my anchor and suddenly it just didn't feel safe anymore. Talking with Jesus didn't feel safe anymore. I think it stopped making sense because I stopped trusting my own ability to know pretty much anything at all. I just started assuming that I was wrong and that I needed to feel and act the same way as these other Christians, but how? I couldn't change the fact that those environments made me painfully scared and uncomfortable. I couldn't force myself to be excited and all-in on those spiritual parties, so was I even a Christian then? Did I even know Jesus? And if I *was* wrong and couldn't get on board with all this spiritual stuff now, then had I ever really known Jesus? or were the past two years just one big lie? Those were the thoughts going on in my head, and I hated every minute of it. I didn't even want to go to church, it pained me to listen to worship music, and reading my Bible didn't feel right. Anyone who knew me would know how insane that was for me. But I didn't want to just sit in that, I wanted to know what was true. I desperately just wanted to know what was right and what was wrong, but unfortunately it was far from black and white and I had about two days before my school started to figure it out. Half of my friends were all for it, and the other half, the half that knew me very well, were not.

I couldn't get myself to not go to school, so there I was bright and early, highly caffeinated, ready to get some answers. For about the first three months of this school, I was on the fence about a whole lot of the teachings they would give. But there was testimony after testimony to back up what they were teaching, so I just kept telling myself to stay teachable.

It was the week before Thanksgiving break that pushed me over the edge and I was faced with a decision to trust my own relationship with God, trust my own discernment and heart, or continue to go with the flow, suck it up, and participate, whether I agreed with it or not. My teacher was going to give a talk on what my church called "manifestations," also known as "why our church is so weird," so I was actually really excited because I felt like I was finally going to get some answers. I wanted to talk with some people I trusted outside of the school about it after, so I decided to record the lecture to make sure I wouldn't be representing it wrong. After the talk, I had the same confusing unsure feeling in my stomach, but I tried to go back to school the next day with an open mind. The next day was when everything went down. Long story short, that day was, from start to finish, the most intense, confusing, and scary day I have ever experienced on a spiritual level. I'm just going to leave it at that. According to my best friend who's house I went to right after, I've never been so distraught before in my life.

It was finally over and we were sent to our small groups where we would discuss what had just happened. I was silent, which if anyone knows me well enough, they know that that is just not normal. When I was finally asked what was wrong, I was told, "Don't worry, someday you'll stop being scared of the Holy Spirit." WHAT?!?! That was the last straw for me. I took a deep breath and, as kindly as I could make it sound, I explained how I knew who Jesus was, how I knew who the Holy Spirit was, and why I very well was not scared of them.

It's crazy because I don't think I realized this at the time, but as I started to speak up in my small group about my own relationship with the Holy Spirit, things got a lot less scary and I felt a lot more powerful over my faith. I felt this new confidence and conviction to stand firm in my own relationship with Jesus, and that I had a responsibility to be bold in that. After getting on my soap box for a hot minute and explaining how when I felt the Holy Spirit for the first time I was overwhelmed by the peaceful, healing, loving presence of Jesus, I realized that I didn't have to doubt my relationship with Jesus after all. I realized that in all of this craziness, my relationship with Jesus was still my relationship with Jesus and nobody was ever going to be able to take that away from me. I realized that it didn't matter whether I knew Jesus for one month, one year, or for my whole life, He loved me just as much as the next person and filled me up with himself without limits. This had nothing to do with me really. This isn't me trying to say that I was smarter or a "better Christian" than these people in my school, this is me saying that I am smarter than I gave myself credit for, but above all else, this is me saying that the closeness I have with Jesus is from Jesus, not because of anything I could know or do. Once I realized that Jesus had been speaking to me and putting convictions in my heart all along, I felt this freedom to stand by that. I felt a freedom that told me that I can't live by someone else's conviction. I can only live by what's true to me, what's authentic for my life, and it just wasn't this.

On November 21st, 2016 I wrote in my journal after this day at school:

"God I believe you speak to me. I believe you perform miracles. I believe that you're going to let into my heart what's right. I don't know if I belong at this school anymore... Do I stay? Maybe it was just for a season? I'm so confused. Both sides are so passionate that they're right- I don't want to pretend. I don't want to fake it. Why was everything so much clearer when I wasn't at the school? Who do I go to? I just want truth. Just like little Amy said, I need to find what's true for me and share that. That's how it's authentic. REAL. The last thing I want to do is put you in a box or pretend I know everything, but this just makes me scared. I was straight up panicking Jesus. Is there something wrong with me because it freaks me out so much? How was it JUST me that was balling my eyes out? WHY was I balling my eyes out? Why do I feel so traumatised? Okay Jesus, you know my heart. I just want to know what's true."

Over Thanksgiving break I had the opportunity to speak with some close leaders that I loved and trusted, who I knew loved and trusted me as well. I showed them the recordings that I had from school, told them about my experience and how it was responded to, and was very validated in my disagreements and uncomforts. Going through Scripture, which I never did nearly as intentionally as I did at this time searching for what was true, I just kept feeling pulled further and further away from my school. But for some reason, I couldn't get myself to fully commit to one side of this. I still kept claiming to be confused, even though deep down I very well knew what I believed and knew was true. But if I knew what was true, why wouldn't I just accept that and move on? Isn't that what I wanted all along? After talking this out with my friend Meg, I was called out on this very issue.

"I don't think you're confused, Jackie, because you really don't sound confused. You sound like you know exactly how you feel, but you're using the word 'confused' because that word feels safe to you. 'Confused' is safe because it's not picking a side. 'Confused' isn't hurting anyone's feelings."

Well, as usual, my friend was right. "Confused" was a safe word for me because it wasn't hurting anyone's feelings. It was a way of me throwing my hands up and not having to pick a side in a fight, even though I knew exactly who I agreed with. Honestly, it's a really scary thing to pick a side in something like this. It felt bold and I really didn't know if I was brave enough to do it. I didn't know that I would have the courage to be in a room full of people that all believed one thing while I believed another, and still stand firm in what I believe. That's a hard thing to do, especially for someone who has the track record of people pleasing that I do. I've always had the mentality where I didn't want to make anyone upset, so just the idea of being the one person to stand up and cause disagreement felt terrifying.

The truth of all this nonsense is that, if I were in a room full of a million people who all thought one way and I thought the other, and what I think is genuine and real to me, that's okay. That doesn't make me wrong. That doesn't make me defected or broken. That just means that what the room full of people think is not genuine to me, and there is nothing in the Bible that says I have to pretend it is to make sure no one gets upset. It's actually *okay* for me to put my foot down and not be part of things that I don't agree with. It's actually so attractive when a person is bold and not afraid of disagreement or conflict that they stand up so firmly for what they believe in, whether they're the only person in the whole world who feels that way or not. I can't live by someone else's conviction. I can't live by what someone else thinks is true, I can only live by what I believe in my heart and what God has revealed to me. I think I've actually been going a little while thinking that disagreement means fighting, anger, or the end of a relationship, but it doesn't. Disagreement actually just means that we're human and we see the world through different eyes. I actually don't think it's possible to find two people that agree one hundred percent on everything in life. All of this just means that we get to have a conversation and that I get to do what's genuine for me, and you get to do what's genuine for you.

So yes, I ended up dropping out of this ministry school that I initially moved across the country for. I don't regret moving, I don't regret trying out the school, and I definitely don't regret my decision to leave because I think I make good decisions. I also know that there are going to be a lot of people out there that disagree with me and, you know what? That's okay. Don't get me wrong, I would love it if we all were on the same page, I just know that's not realistic and that is OKAY. It's better to be firm and bold in what you believe than just sway around and be a chameleon because you're too scared of offending someone. I'm going to let you in on a little secret that took me 22 years to learn; no matter what decision in life you make, no matter how many people agree with you and think you're right, there will always be someone who thinks differently. There will always be someone who gets offended or wants to argue against your point. In the end, disagreement is scary, but it's real. Real is what we want.

I was talking with Amy about these ideas, as I generally tend to do with the big things in my life, and she gave me the most incredible metaphor that has helped her when she has struggled with similar problems. She told me that life is like a big puzzle. Everyone has their own puzzle piece which represents their own experiences and what they know is true about God. The pieces show what God has communicated to them and what God has made real in their hearts. When we start to meet people and get into conversations about what we know is true about God, that's when we get to put our pieces together and see an even clearer picture of what God actually looks like. That's why we need each other, really. But then sometimes we meet someone who's puzzle piece doesn't make sense to us, and we can't quite figure out where it fits. It's when God communicates to people in ways that I'm not going to understand, and I'm not going to know what to do with. But I don't have to pretend to understand, I don't have to live by their puzzle piece, instead I get to live by mine. I do that until I meet more people with more pieces that make the big picture make more sense. The big picture is beautiful, and the big picture is the whole point. That's why we need each other. I think God does this on purpose to bring us together because he knows that. He created us that way.

What I'm trying to say is that I can't judge someone's heart on whether or not they know Jesus just because I don't understand their puzzle piece. My job is to love them and keep chasing after Jesus on my own, and just keep encouraging them to chase after Jesus too. In the end, I absolutely do not know everything. In fact, I know so far from everything,, it's funny. But they don't know everything either! Nobody does, so if you run into someone claiming to have conquered all that mysterious knowledge I would recommend being extremely skeptical. That's why we need Jesus. He's pretty good at knowing things.

I don't want to hide the way I feel anymore. I don't want to not say something because someone somewhere might disagree. I just want to pursue truth and have a conversation about it with other people chasing after the same thing. It took me a lot of debating with myself when I was trying to figure out how to write this section of my book. I knew that this specific section was controversial, and I knew that by putting it in here there were going to be some people who would get upset. There will probably even be people who get offended and say some mean things on twitter or something. I might even get myself some haters. Not to say that the other things I talk about in my book aren't going to be disagreed with, because I'm sure they are, but there was something different that happened in my head when I was writing this one. All of a sudden I started getting scared, and it wasn't because of the vulnerability I was expressing in it, because, let's face it, I pretty much destroyed any illusion of me "having it all together" a long time ago. The reason I was so tempted to take this chapter out was because I knew for a fact there were going to be a lot of people in the Christian community that disagreed with me, and I got scared. Which is totally ironic because of the theme of the chapter anyway, but it was still such a struggle for me to come to terms with.

It's one thing to talk about about being bold, or even write about it for that matter. But when it comes to living that stuff out in the real world, it gets a little intimidating. I knew the point of my book was to be honest and like I've said before, having everyone agree is literally impossible. I realized that if I took this chapter out out of fear of what some people would say, I would be the biggest hypocrite in the world. Well, maybe not the whole world, there's quite a lot of hypocrites out there, but I'd be a big one for sure. With the risk of sounding very "Christianese," I would just like to say that Jesus was beyond controversial, and isn't the goal in life to look more like him anyway? Isn't the goal of this whole Christianity thing to do everything we can to walk and talk and act like Jesus? If it's not, I'd say Christianity sounds like a lame hobby. Read any of the Gospels and really look at the way Jesus acted around the hyper-religious people. They had a million and one rules that they got hyper-offended if someone, especially someone claiming to be God, would break them. Jesus knew their thoughts very well and knew just how wrong they were for feeling that way in the first place, but did he tip toe around their feelings and play by their rules so they wouldn't get upset? Not at all! And thank goodness he didn't because it really wouldn't fit in with the rest of his life or teachings. No, Jesus intentionally went out of his way to offend them because he wanted them to know what was true, and really did not care whether or not they agreed. He wasn't scared of them or how offended they might be, so why should we be? The religious leaders didn't want Jesus to heal the man with the messed up hand on the Sabbath, so what did Jesus do? He healed the man with the messed up hand on the Sabbath. I'm not trying to say that I'm right and they're wrong and that's the end of it; all I'm saying is that when we are convicted on what's true to us, we have a responsibility to live by that truth, *whether people get offended or not.*

Sometimes life gets messy, sometimes there's tension and disagreements, but we get to walk away from all that knowing that God is still good, God is still love, and God is still, and always will be safe.

Relationship

"That's because love is never stationary. In the end, love doesn't just keep thinking about it or keep planning for it. Simply put, love does."

– Bob Goff

AFTER QUITTING MINISTRY SCHOOL I WAS faced with yet again, another transition in 2016. It took a second for it to sink in that, six months prior, I had just uprooted my whole life and moved myself across the country for this reason specifically, and now it was over. About a month or so after I dropped out, I got a phone call from a friend of mine, one that always seems to call when I need her the most, to ask me how I was processing the continuous turn of events. The question caught me a little of guard because it felt like a very intentional thing that needed to be thought about on my end, but I kept trying to avoid for some reason.

Reflecting on the month prior, I couldn't figure out why I felt so funny and "on guard" about it all. I took advantage of the fresh start by moving in with my best friend, going church shopping, getting to know a whole new circle of people, and so on. Everything at this time seemed to be lining up great for me relationally, and I felt like I was supposed to be happier than I was, but I didn't know how to tell my friend why I wasn't.

The more we chatted, the more the truth kind of slapped me in the face. Over the course of 2016, I had moved six times, one being across the country where I restarted every detail of my life without knowing a single soul. Everything in my life kept having a fresh start, and I was getting sick of it. It seemed like every few months I was in a new group of friends, new environment, new town, new culture, new everything, and it was getting really old. The amount of people that came in and out of my life that year was just ridiculous, and even though that's probably a normal part about being in your early 20s, it was just hard. Baggage started to come up from my past, and I was noticing myself feel like I had to protect myself from getting hurt by these, yet again, new friends. As dramatic and Peyton Sawyer-like (for you One Tree Hills fans) as it sounds, I responded to my friend by saying, "People always leave." Wow, there it was. It was sad.

When life goes through the amount of insane transitions as mine did at the time, the most precious thing in the world would be stability. Now that I think about it, I haven't really had much stability in my life since high school. I mean, for all of 2014 when people asked me where I lived, I genuinely didn't know. I was living out of a suitcase and crashing on different tour busses or couches all year. The people I would talk to one night seemed great and all, but what's the point of getting to know them if I'm never going to see them again anyway?

This was sad, but very real. So, as I beat around the bush a bit more on the phone, I finally came to terms with the fact that I was scared of my friends leaving me because, honestly, it would have fit into my story flawlessly. I developed this fear of getting close to people because the closer I would get, the more painful it would be when they all of a sudden got sick of hanging out with me or moved away. That was just flat out depressing, so saying it out loud was pretty embarrassing as well.

I got off the phone and felt pretty mad. I wasn't mad at my friend for asking, I was really just mad that I had these insecurities and fears in the first place. When did this get so bad? The more I thought and journaled about it, I remembered how I felt during that chaotic month in January of 2016 when my community group started kicking me out of Bible study and writing me letters about not being able to be my friend anymore. This was back when I was going to go tell my sister my shame story and really needed my friends' support, but instead, they all bailed after they heard what I had done and chose the other guy's side. I thought about that story, then I thought about how when I told my best friend that her boyfriend raped me when I was 17 and she never talked to me again. Or the time that I moved to LA to hang out with my sister, and ended up crying on the curb instead because she left me to go see her boyfriend. Story after story kept crossing my mind so I picked up one of my old journals when this was going on and read, "I'm starting to come to terms with the fact that at the end of the day, nobody actually cares about me. Nobody will ever actually pick me." Wow. Sad, huh? Well I'm not sure how you're feeling reading this chapter, but as I write it I feel very annoyed and very sick of the idea of my past having a say in my life.

Just because I've been hurt in the past by friends, doesn't mean every friend I have is going to hurt me. Just because I've been left behind before, does not mean I'm going to be left behind right now. That's what's true, and I've now decided that it's about time I start living that way. I get to live a new day, everyday, and give people a new chance everyday as well.

So you want to know what I did? I started opening up about this. Yes, as painfully embarrassing as it was, I was not about to sit in it alone in hopes of it just disappearing. That's just not how it works, and as someone who constantly preaches vulnerability on the internet, it wouldn't make a whole lot of sense for me to do that anyway. That being said, I put on my pjs and crawled into my roommate's bed and told her what was going on in my head. This was hard to do because it just felt annoying, and I felt like by doing this I was risking the thing I was scared of in the first place; her leaving. But if being bold and honest and brave with how I'm feeling is truly what I want to live by, this was absolutely necessary. It was time to put that theory to the test.

"Jackie, I'm not going anywhere."

As simple as those words were, they began to slowly but surely heal that little wound in my heart that I didn't want anyone to see. That right there is community, and that right there is why it is so completely necessary to let yourself be known. The more of me I let my friend know, the more of me I let be loved. Honestly, that's not just community, that's the Gospel. The idea of being fully known and loved anyway is probably the greatest idea that's ever been thought. But even if friends ended up leaving again in the future, I still get to live this way. I still get to wake up in the morning and not be trapped under the assumption that the good things won't last and that people always leave.

Yes, leaving ministry school left me, yet again, in a new season. But I'm learning that that's okay. I'm learning that the amount of control that I have over whether or not things stay the same is very small, and the quicker I learn to be okay with that, the more peaceful my heart is going to be. That being said, I've taken up a new motto from here on out. As I sit in this coffee shop tonight, slightly sad at my empty cappuccino mug, I've decided that when I make a new friend, I'm going to put everything I have into that friendship. When I move to a new home, I'm going to put everything I have into making that home mine. If someone walks out of my life I'm going to remember that, as cliche as it sounds, I have a Father in heaven who knows who I need, and knows when I need them. This might sound naive or a little immature, maybe even dumb depending on your past experiences, but that's just it; past experiences should not have the power to affect us. I'm aware that living this way might get me hurt by some people, but I'm also very aware that by putting my whole heart into my relationships and other aspects of my life, I'm going to experience more fullness and more joy than I ever would have with my guards up. Frankly, I think it's worth the risk.

I have this friend who is honestly one of my favorite people in the whole world. Our typical hobbies involve me putting her on my shoulders, splitting cupcakes in half and eating them in the car on late nights after work, pushing the giant cart together at Costco while we scramble to find all the free samples, and randomly breaking out dancing simultaneously in public. We dance, we laugh, we cry, we do it all. We even go to trampoline parties together. If that's not friendship, who knows what is. This is a friend who has seen more sides and accepted more quirks in me than anyone else in the world. Nothing against anyone else really, I just never let anyone in as close as her for some reason. No one has ever been around me as much as her. She sees me, peanut butter stains and mismatching socks and all, and she just loves me.

I've never lived with a true friend of mine before this point in my life. Don't get me wrong, I've had roommates that I've liked or seen on the occasion, but actually living with someone on the level of closeness that we had was not part of my story until now. I think there's a lot to say about living with people. When I first moved to Nashville I didn't know anyone so I was planning on getting an apartment to myself, which in a lot of ways would be really easy, but in other ways would be flat out sad. Someone's home is their safe place. It's where after a long day at work or a long day with friends, they get to come home, take off their shoes, and just be. Whether that's shutting themselves in their room to stare at the ceiling, reading a book, watching TV shows over a bowl of cereal, or whatever. Home is where if you don't want to talk to anyone and just be a hermit, you're free to do just that.

I think when I moved in with my best friend, I, for the first time, truly understood what it feels like to be known. Not only being known, but sometimes just flat out exposed without a single thing I could do about it. When I'd come home sad, I was seen. When I came home mad, I was seen. Every quirk became noticed, every pattern or habit that I had was on full display. Yes, there's beauty in that. God created us to be known and be in these deep relationships where we can love each other and grow, but the biggest lesson I've learned by this specific friendship is that relationships are just not easy. I think I'm learning more in this best friend/roommate dynamic than I ever did in an actual relationship, because this is the first time someone has seen this much of who I am, good and bad, and hasn't gone anywhere. The only way that's possible in the first place is loads and loads of this little thing called grace.

In a nutshell, I messed up and I did something to upset this friend. At first I really didn't know what I did wrong. I was confused and sad because I knew she was upset but I didn't know why and, in my history with friendships, there have been a few occasions of me doing something to upset someone and the next thing I know the whole relationship goes to shreds. Since this girl is one of my favorite people in the world, the last thing I wanted to do was hurt her. Seeing tears in her eyes and knowing that I caused that absolutely destroyed me. So I was scared, and I felt like I had to prepare myself for some changes in the dynamic. However, the next morning when I woke up, she came to me and explained why she was upset. It was very bold and straightforward, which I wasn't used to by any means because people in my life generally avoided conflict. It was a rare thing when someone came up to me and told me exactly how they felt. After pulling myself together from the shock, I told her I was sorry and expressed where the confusion was. We chatted and she forgave me. Simple as that, no strings attached, she gave me grace. The smoothness of it completely caught me off guard. She reminded me that she still trusted me, still loved me the same, and things were not about to get weird or change in our friendship. Don't get me wrong, I've been given grace before in many different friendships and relationships, but there was something so peaceful and simple about the way this was resolved that I don't think I've experienced before. Receiving this gift from someone who knew me as well as she did, was something special that it's tricky to explain. That's when it hit me, hard. The reason her forgiveness meant more to me than someone else's was BECAUSE she knew me as well as she did. I wasn't giving her some cleaned up pretty version of myself and getting grace for that. No, she got the sometimes not-so-much-fun experience of seeing me with all of my flaws and brokenness exposed. That's not such a pretty sight, people. Let me tell you, the broken self needs a lot more grace than the pretty one does.

I think one of the most important lessons a person can learn in this world is the ability to accept that they're capable of being wrong. Not just that, but also the fact that being wrong isn't the end of the world. I'm definitely not new to this idea about making mistakes (see the whole first half of this book for references), but after the first few confrontations with this friend, because yes there were plenty more to come, it suddenly dawned on me that I'm not perfect and I do in fact have the capability to hurt people. I know what you're thinking; that's crazy! Me? A human being with the ability to hurt someone's feelings?! Nonsense. Well, it became really real to me that day that I do in fact have the ability to hurt people, even when I don't realize it. You can learn a whole lot from living with someone you love. Sometimes when we stick around and fight for a friendship long enough, we even get to learn that people don't always leave. Even when you mess up more than once, sometimes people stick it out with you. I learned that making mistakes doesn't mean that I'm a bad person, a bad friend, or stupid. It just means that I'm human.

The reason these conflicts with my friend were so impactful and difficult for me to accept was genuinely because of how much I cared about her. Since she meant so much to me, the fact that I hurt her really just sucked. But, as I've said before, she continues to forgive me with no strings attached. She doesn't add it to this list of wrongs, doesn't hold a grudge against me, none of that. This friend is probably one of the most forgiving people I've ever had the opportunity of knowing. It's not that she's loud and proud about it, she's just naturally an above and beyond graceful human being, and I'm going to brag on her here as much as I can because this is my book and I can say (almost) whatever I want to. However, the unfortunate thing is that she's been told so many times in her life that to forgive as much and as easily as she does is a bad thing. She's been called a doormat, and been told that this quality is her biggest fault. That right there, that makes me beyond mad. The truth is, by forgiving as unconditionally and as easily as she does, she's actually doing exactly what we're called to do. This isn't her biggest fault, it's actually her greatest quality and biggest strength, and I so admire her for that. The only person who would be at fault in a scenario with her extension of grace would be the one who treats her as a doormat, not her for extending forgiveness. And this girl is someone who has a story of being really, truly hurt by some people in her life. The fact that going through the things she's been through she's still able to pick herself up, keep living by the grace in her heart, and keep assuming the best in people is truly incredible. I'd much rather be a doormat than assume the worst in everyone and cut people out of my life. There's not grace there, which really means that there's not life there either. Why would we let something that someone did a year ago, two years ago, or even last month define who they are today? Would you want someone to define you by what you did a year ago? Do you want someone to bring up something from your past that you're ashamed of and judge you based on that? That's not how relationship works. If grace is what gave us life, then just imagine how much life there will be when we give grace to other people. Grace is the point. The fact that we're forgiven for literally everything we've ever done, when that actually sinks in, it's indescribable. Those moments when you're forgiven and you realize that you don't deserve it, that's when it becomes painfully clear how big of a deal grace is in this world. We can't survive without it, and relationships definitely won't either.

Learning to give grace is one thing, but receiving it is sometimes just as difficult, especially when history proves that grace can sometimes become conditional. As sad as it sounds I really am used to getting cut off when I mess up, but that's not Jesus. I think Jesus would be the person who would stick around. I think Jesus would be the one that hears my story, runs across the room to give me a hug and tell me that he's not going anywhere, and then actually not go anywhere. Jesus would be the one that no matter how many times I messed up, he would just keep forgiving me. He would love me through it so unconditionally that logically, it wouldn't make any sense. But let's be real, there's no "would" with this when it comes to Jesus. All these qualities that my friend has been showing me about grace and love are only possible because they're straight from his heart. That's just how it is. If this girl I've been telling you about reminds you of anyone in your own life, hold onto that person. That person is going to teach you a whole lot about who Jesus actually is.

———

Grace is great and all, *when it's done right*. It sounds pretty to talk about and it's easy on the eyes, but what happens when the person creating the pain doesn't *actually* get it? What if the person doesn't *actually* feel bad, and continues to bring more and more pain to your life, to the point that having them in your life feels purely toxic? Unfortunately, we live in a world where scenarios like this are more common than not. It's just the fact that we're people. Yes, I believe that giving people the benefit of the doubt is huge and so necessary, but the reality is that some of those people end up hurting you in a way that even their presence or the mention of their name brings you pain. Take rape victims, for example. This is an extreme case, but if a girl was being raped by her dad and he apologized but continued to rape her, should she still keep him in her life? Of course not! That story is heartbreaking, but unfortunately we live in a world where the chances of that being the truth in someone's life are pretty great.

I can't speak for anyone else, but in the experiences that I've had receiving grace, it's been nowhere near easy. The reason I felt so bad when my friend extended grace was because the reason behind it in the first place was that I had hurt her. If I really loved her, would I knowingly go back and continue to hurt her? I mean, if she has to give me grace, why not? Why not just do whatever I want if I'm going to be forgiven anyway? That's something that I can't wrap my mind around. But unfortunately we live in a world where there are a lot of people in the Christian culture who view grace that way. The whole relationship aspect with God gets kicked to the curb, and grace goes from a gift out of love from a Father, to a cheap vending machine. If a husband really loved his wife, would he choose to continuously cheat on her? Would he choose to do that then ask for forgiveness only to go back and do it again simply because he could? That logic makes no sense. That's not grace, that's just evil.

Then what do we do when we're hurt so badly by people that the mention of their name gives us shivers down our spines? Yes, I can give you the textbook answer and explain what boundaries are and the proper ways to implement them, but sometimes it's just *not that simple*. Sometimes the people who hurt you really, really hurt you. Sometimes the idea of extending grace towards these people actually feels impossible. Sometimes boundaries feel like a forced bandaid instead of a deeply desired resolution. So, then what?

I had a pretty big fight with someone very close to me recently. Actually, this wasn't even really a fight, this was someone that was supposed to take care of me, but when put in a situation to do so, ended up causing me way more pain than I ever thought was possible. This was a person who left me bawling my eyes out hysterically on an overnight flight back from LA to Nashville. I actually didn't know it was possible to cry that hard for so long without being able to control myself. I know this sounds sad and all for me, but just think about how awkward the poor passengers on my row felt. I mean, there was snot flying and so many hiccups. It was *that bad*. This was a person who, at my waitressing job, left me dropping my stack of trays and running to the trashcan to throw up after glancing at his text message. My world was spinning and there didn't seem to be one person who didn't know it. I felt like one glance in my eyes and I was automatically exposed. I was still new to Nashville at the time, so I didn't really have too many people I felt like I could go to this with which just sucked, for lack of better words. I was just lonely to the core.

So what did I do? I shut him out. I went into full on defense mode and was completely torn up about it for months on end. I was so terrified of getting hurt again that even the thought of letting this person back into my life felt impossible. As if the trauma wasn't enough, the anger I felt at this person was plenty of a burden on its own. I would vent and vent about how much this person needed to apologize, but the truth was that even if he did, I was nowhere near ready to forgive him. Deep down I didn't want him to apologize because I didn't want to be put into the position to have to forgive him. I didn't want to have to be the bigger person. That's how mad I was. I prayed and I prayed and all I wanted was peace. All I wanted was for this to go away.

When it comes to the topic of forgiveness, I have a lot of thoughts. What I know to be true is that forgiveness is a choice. Forgiveness isn't so much for the other person as it is for you, and what happens on the other side of genuine forgiveness is life and freedom. But what happens in the middle of it when, no matter how many times you say it out loud, the anger doesn't go away, nor does the peace feel any closer? I think forgiveness is beautiful, don't get me wrong, but I also think that there's a version of forgiveness that doesn't work. I say that because I've experienced the real version, and when someone comes into contact with what's real, it becomes obvious when something isn't.

I was at that ministry school still during the time that this was going on. The topic for that week at school was, of course, forgiveness. Session after session of hearing why we need to forgive, how much we were forgiven for, and what forgiveness even means, I was still in the same boat as before. We had to stand up, say a prayer all together claiming to forgive this person and that person, sit down, then stand up and do it all over again. I did it because I was told to and it would have been incredibly awkward for me to not participate in this, but this was truthfully a very ungenuine thing for me to do. I'm not expert on the subject and could be completely wrong here, but there really wasn't anything in my heart that felt freedom after simply stating the words "I forgive..." over and over again, and I can't imagine them helping someone else in a situation like or worse than mine either.

Then again, who am I to judge what forgiveness looks like or feels like? I'm talking about one of the greatest ideas in the world here. Forgiveness is why you and I are still living right now. It's why we have hope for anything good in the world. All I'm saying is that I was confused. Does forgiveness come after the pain? Before the pain? Do we have to verbally tell someone, "I forgive you," in able to actually forgive them?

During this internal argument I was having with myself, I started talking to my friend Amy Pape. Amy always seemed to have some mysterious way of making really complicated problems in my life more manageable, while helping me feel less alone in the process. She told me that she sees forgiveness as inviting Jesus into the pain with you. It's a way of saying, "hey I'm still hurt, but I want freedom from the hurt." *Forgiveness was never meant to be a solo job.* There's really not a lot in this life that is.

Please don't feel shame if your heart doesn't feel ready and healed up to forgive. If you can't let go of anger at someone who deeply wronged you, it just means that you're human. It doesn't mean you're this evil person who is stuck in a hopeless pile of pain, it just means that you're no different than me or the next person. All this means is that we need Jesus. As simple and cliche as that sounds, it's really the only way it works. I'm only saying this because these are things that I was feeling at this time in my life. I thought I was going to grow up to be a bitter old lady if I didn't figure this out. I knew my heart and I was ashamed that I wasn't able to feel the freedom it seemed like the rest of my friends were feeling that day at school. I don't have all the answers to this, so I'm sorry if you had your hopes up about the end of this chapter, but I can tell you that forgiveness is a decision, a process, and something that really can't be done alone. I can tell you that at the end of this process, freedom will come.

Insecure

"Love yourself first, and everything else falls into line. You really have to love yourself to get anything done in this world."

– Lucille Ball

"Adolescence is just one big walking pimple."

– Carol Burnett

OKAY, SO THIS CHAPTER IS GOING TO BE A tough one to write. This one is about something that I don't talk about like, ever, because it's honestly just embarrassing. But I know that I have to put it in here because it's what's true and that is what has power. That being said, for pretty much my whole life I've struggled with body image issues. Shocker, right? I mean, I'm a girl. Not to stereotype us or anything like that ladies, but I'm not going to pretend like body image issues aren't a common thing for women. It sucks, but it's true.

I think the first time I remember looking in the mirror and not liking what I saw was when I was in the seventh grade. I'm just going to lay it all out for you, okay? There was this boy at school that I liked. Honestly he was kind of a jerk and I knew it, but I liked him because he had cool flippy hair and wore board shorts and puka shell necklaces. Anyway, word on the school bus was that this guy happened to like me as well. Little 13-year-old Jackie was absolutely thrilled. Before we knew it, text messages were being exchanged and sparks were flying like a Nicholas Sparks novel. But all of a sudden he stopped texting me, and a few days later I got a phone call. I picked up to his friend and himself laughing and telling me that I had, "thunder thighs," and that my other friend was, "like ten times hotter." I thought that was the end. I had never felt a feeling like that in the pit of my stomach before. I just wanted to crawl in a hole and never come out so that nobody would have to see my ugly body again.

That's when it all started. Looking back now I know that I was in no way overweight. I know that they were just dumb kids, but my pain was real. I started spitting out the food I was eating at dinner into my napkin, started waking up at five in the morning to do aerobics before school, went on weird diets where I would eat things like three saltine crackers and half a cup of cottage cheese... all sorts of stuff. I would avoid going to the bathroom with all my girlfriends in between classes because I didn't want to have to stare at myself in the mirror and compare myself to them while they fixed their hair for 20 minutes. Actually, if I'm being *really* honest, I pretty much avoided mirrors at all costs. Pictures and videos as well, which is so sad now because I love videos! I just became obsessed with trying to be the skinny girl. I thought that's what would make boys like me or girls want to be my friend. I would *obsess* over my body, and when I finally felt confident in how I looked, I would stress over losing that so the pressure to eat practically nothing became even bigger.

Going out to eat with friends was the absolute worst too. The last thing in the world I would have ever wanted to happen was for people to find out about what I was doing. As I got older and started to live on my own, my grocery shopping list was literally apples, bananas, peanut butter, and cereal. For a while, those were the only things I felt comfortable eating which doesn't even make sense now. I would literally survive off of that and occasionally two bites of whatever my close friends were eating.

I didn't like doing that by any means. It was embarrassing because it was becoming obvious. I would turn down offers of food like it was my hobby, and people would start to ask. I'd spend hours on hours at the gym, but actually start to hate myself if I had a bite of a cookie. I think I just wanted control to be honest, because I wasn't fat. I really wasn't, but for some reason I was just terrified. If I ate a whole meal for dinner, I felt like I failed. If I ate nothing, I was proud.

I'm not really sure how this stopped because I honestly didn't think it would. I used to write in my journals and pray that God would take it away and let me be normal with food, so maybe he did? I was embarrassed and I was scared. I'm at a place right now that I never really thought I would be at. I'm confident in my body and I know how to act in my own skin, and I'm proud of that. For anyone out there reading this that has ever struggled with an eating disorder, I'm not going to quote Scripture here or tell you that, "God made you and God doesn't make mistakes," or any of those cliche Christian one-liners that get thrown around on bumper stickers and coffee mugs. Yes, I do believe them with my whole heart, but I know that throwing those Scriptures around isn't going to fix people. What I am going to tell you is that there is hope. You are beautiful, whether you believe me or not. The reason I shared this part of my story here is simply because I need you to know that if you have those scary thoughts about your body, you're not alone. There's no isolation in that, and if you feel it then you need to trust me when I tell you that it's a lie.

I'm actually writing this chapter after watching an older Coffee Chats with Jax video where I opened up about my body image issues on the internet. I remember making that video and not knowing how to end it. I wanted to give a solution but I didn't have one, so I gave a Bible verse. That's it. I'm not saying the Bible verse is wrong, but I'm not happy with how I ended that video. Instead of just staying vulnerable and being there with the people watching, feeling the fear and pain with those in the same struggle, I got uncomfortable and wanted to tie a pretty bow at the end with some Jesus to show people that I was fine. The Scripture wasn't wrong, but I was wrong for hiding behind it. So I decided that I needed to try again here, and ask for forgiveness for that. This is me being real with you and telling you that sometimes just hearing Scripture doesn't fix things. I think sometimes maybe, just maybe, God wants us to sit with each other and just be real with where we're at. He wants us to open up about what we're feeling and not put a verse on it in hopes of nobody finding out the truth. So you know what guys? Body image issues suck. They're scary and lonely, and I really hope that those out there reading this just take away that they're not alone.

Life

*"I think if you can dance and be free and not
embarrassed, you can rule the world."*

– Amy Poehler

WHEN I WAS A LITTLE GIRL, I WAS OBSESSED
with every type of animal out there. I'm talking bugs, rodents, dogs,
fish, cows, you name it. My best friend Maddi and I used to stay
inside from recess to do voluntary research projects on different dog
breeds. We would camp out in the media center at the animal section
and just go to town. For show-and-tell we would bring in our ham-
sters to spend the day with us, and build them the coolest cardboard
houses with furniture and a fully stocked refrigerator. It was a great
time.

When I was six years old, I used to collect rolly pollies. Yes,
rolly pollies as in those little black bugs that curl up into a ball if they
get scared or when they go to sleep. I would spend day and night dig-
ging them up and sticking them into my little buckets with dirt tun-
nels and dandelions, then sit in my garage with them to make sure
they were all getting along and no one was getting left out. Then one
day I got a business plan in my little six-year-old entrepreneur mind,

and I decided I would take my rolly polly friends and sell them door to door for a quarter a piece. To make my business start off strong, I knew I was going to have to get up extra early the next morning to stock up on my supply so I asked my dad if he would wake me up at five in the morning sharp. Due to the fact that he would as well have to wake up that early in order to help me up, he wasn't so thrilled about the plan so he told me to just ask God to do it for me instead. Thinking back on this story today, I know that my dad was just trying to get me to leave him alone about the potential early morning I was threatening him with, but back then I took him very literally.

Getting on my knees by my bed that night, I prayed and asked God to wake me up at 5am so I could go expand my rolly polly inventory. As a little girl, there was not a single doubt in my mind that God was going to wake me up, especially after my dad told me to ask. Just as easy as it was for me to believe Santa Claus would bring me presents on Christmas day, I believed that I was going to get a wake up call from Jesus the next morning. Next thing you know my little eyes peeled open, I glanced over at my bedroom clock that read exactly 5am. I thought nothing of it and threw on my pink raincoat and headed outside to fill my bucket with bugs for the day.

The cool thing about this was that the whole next day as I was collecting my rolly pollies and ringing doorbell after doorbell trying to convince my neighbors that they needed one of my products to make their lives better, all I could think about was, "Wow, God is real! That's so cool." That's what I believed, and there's not one person who could have proven to me otherwise at six years old. I was convinced.

Lately I've been hearing a lot about how important it is to have this little thing called "childlike faith." Hearing that over and over again, my mind keeps going back to this memory of me collecting my bugs. In one sense, this story is really no big deal, right? It's literally just a story about a young girl waking up at five in the morning and starting a surprisingly successful bug business. But in another since, this story is a picture of one of the most beautiful, precious things in the whole world. This was the first day that I was shown that God was real. This was the day that little six-year-old Jackie was gifted with the faith for God to show himself to me. I think childlike faith is much simpler than we make it seem sometimes. That's the beauty of it. When someone tells a little kid that Santa is real, the kid is most likely going to believe them. If a kid's dad tells him to trust him, the kid is most likely going to trust his dad. There's even those absolutely adorable cases where you see a little boy wake up with his dad before work to watch him get ready for the day, and mirror everything he does to try to be like him. I think that's how God wants us to be with him. When he tells us the truth, whether that's through the word or through worship and prayer, he wants us to trust him. When we need help with something, anything really even if it's as little as waking up early to catch some bugs, he wants us to go to him. He wants us to wake up early to spend time with him, then try to act like he acts simply because he's our dad.

Next time you're around a kid or two, maybe it's your own or maybe it's one at the table next to yours in a restaurant, pay attention. Not in a creepy way to where the parents are assuming you're some kind of sick kidnapper or something, but in a subtle way look at how the kid interacts with his parents. Look at how he depends on them for literally everything. That relationship can be your best teacher when it comes to God. It takes humility, yes, but I think that those relationships we see between a young child and his parents are what God wants from us as well.

~~~

I think I eat cereal for dinner five out of the seven nights a week. I'm not even talking about the fun kind of cereal, I eat old lady bran. I fill up my oversized *Friends* themed coffee mug with my Fiber One original bran flakes, throw in a packet of stevia to satisfy my constant craving for sweets and just go to town. Usually it's in front of a TV show around 12:30 AM. I can't believe I'm telling you this, how embarrassing.

I'm also weirdly obsessed with going to the grocery store. Whether it's an extended trip to restock my entire pantry (which I rarely do because that would mean I wouldn't get to go back again the next day) or just picking up a carton of milk, I get pretty excited about it. I'm not sure if there's something comforting about strolling up and down the different aisles, or the potential chances of free samples in the bakery section, but I just can't get enough of it. There's actually a couple close friendships that I have that started in the grocery store. I'm not sure if we would have connected as well if it wasn't for the cereal aisle. Not a lot of people understand that side of me. "It's as if you've never seen the inside of a store before Jackie," is a common response I get when I let someone into my weirdness. But what really doesn't make sense about this side of me is that anyone who REALLY knows me knows that I pretty much live off of about five groceries: apples, peanut butter, bananas, cereal, and Quest bars.

Yep, that's me. So why do I need to go to the grocery store everyday? The world will never know.

If you haven't noticed already, I get really excited about the Disney Channel. I have all my life, and I don't think that's going to change, nor do I want it to. I used to get up at 4:50am when I was in middle school so that I could work out to my mom's aerobics tape, shower, and get as many episodes of Lizzie McGuire in before I had to leave for the bus. I was really dedicated. I still watch those old shows now and I'm 22. I might not be as loyal as to get up at 4:50 in the morning, but I still watch them. If you don't believe me, just ask any of the twenty six roommates I've had this past year.

These are some facts about me that sound funny when I talk about them and might even get a giggle or two depending on either your sense of humor or how well you know me by now. They're little quirks that make me who I am, and I'm starting to learn that there's a lot to be said about being proud of that. I've gone through different waves of being extremely confident in myself, to being more insecure than I knew what to do with. I'm not sure why exactly that happens, I'm sure there's some sort of spiritual answer to this but right now I'm just going to call it being a human. I think if we take out all the complicated nonsense from a lot of problems in life, being human might end up being the answer to more than we thought. If being human is the answer, which we all are, then maybe we should stop being so hard on each other. Clearly being human is something we can all relate to (unless you're some kind of dog that learned to read).

You know that cheesy inspirational quote that was probably on some poster in your third grade class that says, "Be yourself, everybody else is already taken"? Well I think that has more power than we've given it credit for. When I think about the moments where I'm the most insecure about who I am, I tend to act out by trying to be like the people in my life. Whether that was trying to look and act like my big sister growing up, attempting to fit in with my friends today as a grown up, or even changing my eating habits or sense of humor preferences to match someone else's. I'm not sure why, but this realization hit me the other night on the couch while I was eating my nightly bowl of bran in front of an episode of *How I Met Your Mother*. I felt like I was coming face to face with who I was, quirks and all, and I was just okay with it. It's not that I wasn't before, I just didn't feel the freedom to embrace it with as much confidence as I'd want to. There was always someone who I felt I needed to be like or earn the applause of. There's plenty of things wrong with that, which I am fully aware of, but for right now I want to talk about the whole "applause" thing.

Unfortunately, we live in a world where people get a little too excited when they gain a few followers on Instagram. It's a world where there's a major difference between a hundred likes on a post versus fifty. Status is a pretty big deal these days, and living in a city like Nashville or LA, it's a pretty loud and in-your-face kind of thing.

But what if we're wrong? What if the defining aspects of a person actually had nothing to do with their social media following or the brand of shoes they wear? What if we had it backwards this whole time? What if it was true what they said in high school about how the geeks were going to make a comeback someday and all the jocks and cheerleaders will hit their peaks at 20-years-old? I think that actually might be my biggest pet peeve about living in Nashville. There's too many people overly concerned about who knows who,

who wears what and how many views they got on their Snap story. I'm sure it's not just Nashville, it just seems to be more flashy here. LA had its own version of that, but the difference was that LA was pretty known and confident in its superficial vibe. Nashville is part of this thing called the Bible Belt, and the Bible Belt has a bad habit of pretending to be better and nicer than it actually is. I'm sorry if this sounds harsh, it's just that if one more person tells me about their Instagram follower count, I might have to throw something.

Donald Miller worded this beautifully in his book Scary Close.

"What if we are designed as sensitive antennas, receptors to receive love, a longing we often mistake as a need to be impressive? What if some of the most successful people in the world got that way because their success was fueled by a misappropriated need for love? What if the people we consider to be great are actually the most broken? And what if the whole time they're seeking applause they are missing out on true intimacy because they've never learned how to receive it?"

I find it pretty ironic that the most famous, successful people sometimes end up being the most unhappy. For example, men like Robin Williams, who committed suicide. That sort of thing makes me question the method through which the majority of society seeks happiness. At the end of the day, who are we all trying to be? What are we all trying to do?

Someone was telling me a story once about a time when she was younger and had this friend who pretty much just marched at the beat of her own drum. This was someone who I don't think a lot of people wanted to be around or have as their friend because she was so "different." She was just one of those dreamers who had her own style and really just didn't care what everyone else's two cents about it were. So my friend was telling me that when she saw this girl, she knew that she had to be her friend. She knew that there was just something that this girl had in life that she needed more of. So what ended up happening was that this girl ended up putting on a one woman show for my friend. I'm talking a full on monologue, most likely with props.

The cool thing about this story is that what was going through my friend's head the whole time this was happening, was that if Jesus came back today, just showed up out of the blue and told everyone, "Hey guys, I'm Jesus. I'm the way to live life. Drop everything that you have, everything that you know, and follow me. I have an idea for your life." If Jesus came and did that, the person that would follow would, hands down, be the girl performing the skit. It would be the girl marching to the beat of her own drum, the girl who didn't care what anyone else thought. She's the one who would follow Jesus, she's the one who would drop everything and be all-in.

That conversation I had with my friend when I learned about this incident with the monologue girl was a pretty quick chat, but it stuck with me for a while. I think there's a deeper purpose behind that. In fact, I think there's a deeper purpose behind most things that stick with you when you don't really know why.

One of the reasons this story might have stuck out to me was because it reminded me of the book in the Bible that I believe saved my life, 1 Corinthians. In the first chapter of that book, the chapter that totally blew my mind two years ago, Paul talks about how God makes the wisdom of the world look foolish. It says, "I will discard the wisdom of the wise and discard the intelligence of the intelligent." In other words, we have it all backwards. The cool kids might not actually be that cool, and the rich people might not actually be that rich. There's just something so remarkable about the fact that Jesus chose, out of all the animals in the world, a donkey to ride on for his big day. By all means he's Jesus, he very well could have chosen some majestic award winning stallion, but he chose an animal two steps down from a miniature horse. There's a reason that Jesus didn't come as some big shining king. There's a reason he came as a carpenter's son. There's a reason that the disciples that he chose were teenage boys. Guys, come on now, teenage boys. He literally had the world at his fingertips and he chose a bunch of teenage boys to be his crew. They weren't big names, they weren't famous bloggers with a bunch of Instagram followers, they were just *boys*. The reason I'm pointing all this out, well one of them anyway, is to make it clear that Jesus didn't seem to care about status. Jesus didn't seem to care about having the fanciest ride on his way into town or the most stylish boy-band-looking group of friends to hang out with. In my eyes, and probably yours too, this doesn't make a lot of sense. Why did Jesus choose the things that he chose if they didn't have any real significance or value? Or did they? If Paul knew what he was talking about when he wrote his section of the Bible (and my money's on him knowing), then you and I might not actually be as wise as we think. What exactly was Jesus' motive behind choosing who and what he chose? I'm not going to pretend to have the answer because I really don't. But my guess is that he knew something that we didn't about what it means to be significant, and I don't think it had the slightest thing to do with who followed who on Instagram.

———

"Becoming a Christian is more like falling in love than understanding a series of ideas or concepts." Donald Miller wrote those words in his book *Searching for God Knows What*, and they've done a pretty decent job leaving a mark on my life thus far. As I've said before, I didn't really start to follow Jesus until about two years ago. So if I would have seen this quote before that, I would be completely lost and confused. Christianity just seemed like any old religion to me and judging by things from the culture I lived amongst, I'm not very surprised that I used to feel that way. I had heard the Christian lingo and the different theological debates, but I didn't actually know God. I knew different things about him, sure, but I didn't know the first thing about what a relationship with God was actually supposed to feel like.

I visited my friends in LA last weekend and the whole trip was absolutely amazing because the friends that I'm talking about are more like family. They are, without a doubt, some of the most supportive human beings that I've ever met. I'm not just saying that because they're my friends, I'm saying that because it's the truth and I think the world can learn a lot about love by just watching them for a second. While I was in LA, I started to feel a handful of different emotional things that I haven't really thought about for a while. At first I just assumed I had missed my friends and my heart forgot how to handle the excitement, which can very well be true, but there was something deeper going on there. The first morning I woke up in their apartment and I sat outside on the fire escape and drank my coffee. I wanted to journal, but I felt like all I could do was stare at the city. It wasn't even currently a pretty thing to look at, it was a bunch of cars and smog and horns and potential parking tickets. But all I could do was stare, and the longer I stared, the longer I loved everything about it.

There's a special kind of wonder and innocence about Jesus in LA. It's the kind of wonder that can't really be found in the Bible Belt with a church on every corner and a Christian bookstore at arms reach always. It's the kind of wonder that swept me off my feet the two years that I called that city home. I think a huge reason there's this special innocence is because Jesus isn't exactly casual conversation out there. LA is full of brokenness, same as every other city whether it's in the Bible belt or not, but LA knows it. I think the reason people are more innocent and open to hearing about Jesus there is because they really know that they need him. Of course there's brokenness everywhere, but when you're just miles away from places like skid row or West Hollywood's strip clubs, the brokenness stares you in the face a little harder and I have a difficult time ignoring that.

When I lived in LA, conversations about Jesus were a constant, everyday thing in my life that I absolutely adored. I was hungry for them, and so were the people I surrounded myself by. I didn't grow up in church so I was fortunate enough to not have the baggage that a childhood with that came with, so I was open and excited for just about everything. If someone in LA loved Jesus, you knew it. If someone didn't actually love Jesus, they weren't going to pretend to. People just were who they were. I'm not naive to the fact that there's also plenty of superficial aspects to the city where Hollywood resides and everyone wants their big break, but LA is a big place and I was fortunate enough to see both sides of that story.

When I moved to Nashville, I honestly had no idea what I was getting myself into. Being a newer Christian, the idea of living in the Bible Belt with a church on every corner sounded like pure bliss to me. Going to a ministry school where everyone uses the same language and such seemed to me like Disneyland. I said Disneyland people, churros and all! I seriously couldn't think of anything better, but I also thought I had it under control. I thought I knew exactly what it was going to look like and how much I was going to love it. I mean, worship every morning, prayer rooms, sermons everyday, how could anything go wrong there? Ha. If someone were to tell me that I was going to end up dropping out of ministry school, questioning everything about my faith and Christianity that I've ever known, and not wanting to go to a church or hear what people had to say about their church in the slightest bit, I never would have believed them.

It was about a year ago this time when I was planning all of this out. All I could think about, talk about, and dream about was Nashville. I spent hours on end reading and re-reading everything on the school website, pinning pinterest post after pinterest post of the top things to do in Nashville and where/what to eat, you name it. My body still resided in LA, but everything in my heart and brain was pleading for Tennessee. I remember waiting to cross the street in Old Town Pasadena with my dear friend Amy Pape after one of our many incredible conversations in a coffee shop, and she told me something that I didn't really understand the depth of or believe until now.

"Jackie, you can go to this school and learn so much and absolutely love it, but you need to know that you already have all the tools that they're going to teach you. Your relationship with Jesus is already incredible, you don't NEED this school to give you anything more for that than you already have. You're already there. Remember that. "

I don't think I really believed her. I appreciated it and was encouraged as always, but I don't think my heart actually accepted what she said as truth yet. I thought this school was my ticket. I brought up this conversation we had at that crosswalk in Pasadena the other night with her while I was visiting, and couldn't help but notice how amazing that girl is at loving me exactly where I'm at. She loved and encouraged me during my over the top excitement before, during my process while I was there, and even now when I'm all dropped out and processing the leftover confusion on why I was there to begin with. It hasn't changed.

Another thing that happened a year ago, which is truly an accurate time span because it came up on my Timehop today (and Timehop doesn't lie) was a road trip. Amy Pape and I were sitting at The Cheesecake factory in Pasadena getting dinner and cheesecake (*of course*) and we were just casually planning out our weekend when we both discovered we had nothing to do.

"Want to drive to Redding to see Bethel?" I asked.

"Sure," Amy answered.

"Wait... really?"

"Let's do it."

The beginning of that story seems like it should be longer, but that is oddly enough an accurate representation of what happened. I had always heard about the church Bethel and always had these dreams of seeing it for myself, so given this opportunity I was all for it. We asked a few people to join us, but no one else was in the mood for an out-of-the-blue seven-hour car ride, so we hit the road by ourselves.

I was so excited. Like so above and beyond excited to see this church, it almost didn't make any sense. What was I expecting to find? What was I expecting to discover when we got there? This church was really built up in my mind and getting to go there actually felt like a dream.

While we were there it was absolutely stunning. The outside was gorgeous, there was a cafe built in, amazing worship, a great message... I seriously had no complaints. It was the first time I had ever experienced worship that lasted for an hour but felt like five minutes, so there's that. I loved it, but it felt strange.

After the service and chatting was done, I was having some time alone in the prayer room to talk to Jesus, journal, and just process what was going on in my head. While I was sitting there, I took a step back and realized that the reason I felt so strange was because I was feeling weirdly convicted for something that I couldn't exactly put my finger on. Being excited is one thing, but I don't think I should have been *that* excited. That's when it hit me. I was glorifying the people at this church. I had these false expectations on what this church and these people were capable of doing for me and it wasn't okay. It was as if I was going there expecting to find God, like that was where God was and I had to get there to get him. The thing is, I have God with me every single day. I have God with me in my car, on my couch, at church, at school, at work, you name it. I have him everywhere I go, as much as I need him, and that right there is never going to change. Nothing against Bethel, it just wasn't the answer to my problems. I think if we look deep enough, there might be a lot of things that we accidentally glorify in life that we shouldn't. The problem with doing that is that because no one and nothing on Earth is actually perfect, we will forever get let down. Not even just in a church environment, just in life. What happens when a girl is so desperate to get married that she ends up pleading and searching for a husband everywhere she goes. She thinks THAT is what will solve her problems, THAT is what will complete her. So then she meets the guy that seems perfect and she freaks out about it. Easily understandable, being a girl myself and also been under the assumption that I have met a perfect guy before, it's just never going to be true. Whether or not this guy is amazing, they get married, have all the kids and live happily ever after, somewhere in the midst of the fairytale disappointment will arise. I'm sorry to burst your bubble girls, but the guy is not going to fix your problems or be everything that you need. Neither will the job you have your hopes up for. Disappointment is inevitable, but that's okay! We're human. We make mistakes regularly and that is why people make terrible gods. That is why jobs and marriages and churches make terrible gods. They're all gifts really, and hopefully will be used to show us more of who Jesus is, but if the glory is given to the creation instead of the creator, we will always end up disappointed. That goes for Bethel, that goes for the smallest church in the world, for Hillsong, for your favorite boy band, and even for your highschool crush.

This isn't meant to bash church, which I certainly hope is not how it's coming across. But this is just me learning that church in itself is not the answer to my problems; Jesus is. Church is ran by people, and people are, believe it or not, not perfect. God doesn't need a mega church like Bethel to move. God can move through any person he wants to, in any situation he wants to. It was during this experience that, for the first time, I understood that just because I move to Nashville that does not mean God is going to love me or show up any more than I would if I had stayed in LA. Yes, things like moving to Nashville are a gift, places like Bethel is a gift, but neither of those things will ever be big enough to be the answer to my problems. Whether I'm standing up in church raising my hands in worship or sitting in my room alone watching Netflix, God loves me just as much. Realizing that was like a Christmas present. There's nothing you can do, and there's nowhere you can go that will make God love you any more than he already does. That's a weird thing for us to understand because it's a normal and understood thing in life that if you work hard, you'll get to where you want to go. If you study hard in school, you'll get good grades. If you work hard at your job, you'll make good money. Life is sadly based a little more on performance than is healthy, in my opinion. But the thing is, when it comes to God, it's done. We don't have to go anywhere or do anything to make that happen. Yes, God told me to move to Nashville. So I think it's a pretty big deal that I moved here. But if I didn't move, his love for me would have looked the exact same. That is not because of anything that I could do or will do, it's all because of what Jesus already did and I think that's beautiful.

I think it's time we stop stressing out about what it is that is God's will for our life. God is so huge, so grand, so divine that in our wildest and craziest dreams, we will never fully understand how amazing he is. If we can understand God, then we're putting him in a little tiny baby box. That's not a God that I would want to serve. This is all based on trust. It's trusting how much God loves us. It's not about how much we love God, because I'm going to love God as much as I can, but I know that eventually I'm going to fail at that. I'm going to be the nicest I can, as selfless as I can, but I'm going to mess up at some point because the best we can is just always going to fail. We're human. I'm aware that sounds pessimistic, but it's the truth. But you know what's not going to fail? Jesus' love for us. That's why we need him. That's why he's the answer. It's when we trust that in our hearts that we get peace. It's when we look at ourselves and how broken we are that we realize that we really don't have any other options. Where else could we go?

I think this lesson that I learned on my seven hour road trip to Redding was preparing me for the lesson I learned a year later during my time in Nashville. It looks different and it's a bit more drawn out, but the point is I'm loved. I'm loved in LA, I'm loved in Nashville, I'm loved in the school, I'm loved after dropping out of the school. I'm loved, and so are you. That's the point.

Amy Pape was right when we were at that crosswalk in Pasadena. I already had everything I needed. In fact, I was born with it. What I needed was Jesus' heart, and that's something no school or new city can give me. God bless you, Amy Pape.

I'm at the point in my journey of writing this book where it's really starting to hit me about what I'm actually doing. The cool part is that I'm more confident and feel more purposeful doing this than I ever expected, but the not-so-cool part is that it feels really scary at the same time. In Donald Miller's book *Scary Close*, he talks about his experiences of writing and how it made him feel getting his *Blue Like Jazz* book as a best-seller. Once that book hit the charts as well as it did, there was a pressure he felt to keep writing best sellers. It was almost like there was a fear that nothing he would write would be as good as that, so he would hide away in cabins for months at a time trying to write the next best thing. Not to give too much away about the book Scary Close, because if you haven't already, please do yourself a favor and put this down for a minute to pick that one up, but the lesson Don learned from hiding away in cabins was that it wasn't okay. His wife Betsy taught him that it's not his best selling books that make him loved, it's himself. It's his heart, who he is, and that he's good for people. Don was getting his identity by writing books and his world was totally flipped when Betsy showed him another way.

Not to say that I'm writing a best-selling book here or anything, I just, for a moment, began to feel a bit of that pressure that Don was talking about. I let a couple of my really close friends, the family kind of friends, read through a draft of my book. After they read it and told me about how it impacted them, I felt something that I've never felt before. First of all, I've pretty much bared my whole heart and soul for you guys here. I mean, I'm not sure how much is going to stay to the final draft or not, but as of right now, I've never been so vulnerable in my entire life. I know it's just on my computer at the moment, but that's tough stuff. It's a weird feeling. Honestly, I expected it to feel scarier than it was, but I lucked out with who I got to share it with. If I've ever been able to say that I completely and fully trust someone without the slightest fears of that being broken, it would be with the girls that read my draft. So it felt safe. Exposing, but safe. I kind of just felt like I didn't have any secrets anymore, like I had a couple more encouraging voices in my head assuring me that, regardless of anything that I've done in my life or thought, I'm still okay.

Anyway, I guess the whole vulnerability side of it surprised me a bit. I know I preach about it pretty much daily on the internet, and have written about it plenty already, but just in case you read that part in the middle of a cookie butter day dream, here's another reminder that it's worth it. When it's with people you trust, being known and loved is, well, the opposite of loneliness. Since I fully agree with Marilyn Monroe about loneliness being my least favorite thing about life, finding the opposite feels pretty good.

Okay, the point of all this is that I got some very good responses from my friends who read my book. They didn't just feel like comments meant to butter me up or anything either, they were straight up honoring. Once I let people into this book writing journey and got feedback, the project suddenly felt bigger than me. It wasn't just this fun little thing I was doing on the side and felt proud of because hey, how many other people can answer the, "what have you been up to?" question with, "I'm writing a book!" It became a real thing that someday people were going to read and be affected by. My life, my story, my mistakes, they suddenly mattered a little more than I thought they did.

It's an interesting feeling, you know? Writing a book and all. My mom used to tell me when I was little that I should be a writer. I didn't want to hear it, all I wanted to do was train dolphins and hunt dinosaurs part-time. Writing didn't seem nearly as exciting, so every time she brought it up I just shrugged it off and went back to Tyrannosaurus Rex research. Sidenote: I'm really happy Google knows how to spell Tyrannosaurus Rex because I had no idea. I probably wouldn't have made a very good dinosaur hunter.

"Writers don't make any money at all. We make about a dollar. It is terrible. But then again we don't work either. We sit around in our underwear until noon then go downstairs and make coffee, fry some eggs, read the paper, read part of a book, smell the book, wonder if perhaps we ourselves should work on our book, smell the book again, throw the book across the room because we are quite jealous that any other person wrote a book, feel terribly guilty about throwing the schmuck's book across the room because we secretly wonder if God in heaven noticed our evil jealousy, or worse, our laziness. We then lie across the couch face down and mumble to God to forgive us because we are secretly afraid He is going to dry up all our words because we envied another man's stupid words. And for this, as I said, we are paid a dollar. We are worth so much more."

– Donald Miller

Don said it pretty well. Writers are superheroes. They're a lot more exciting than dinosaur hunters.

I'm not sure what changed in me to bring me to this place. I don't think it was sudden, but I do think it was intentional. And being as intentional as I know that God is, I know that the timing is now, and the timing is perfect for me to do this. But yes, being real with you would in fact mean that I should tell you that it's terrifying. There's thoughts and stories and mistakes that I've made that are now permanently in this book that someday will be on display for the world to see. It's not like I can publish it then change my mind and franticly smudge white out over the awkward and embarrassing parts in every copy I can get my hands on. Whether two people pick this up and read it, whether just my mom buys a copy, it's available nonetheless. Since I feel the conviction in my heart that it has purpose and it needs to be written, I feel pressure to get it done. I've had the thoughts in my head that Don mentioned about only being worthy if this book is great. Thoughts like I'm only going to be loved and worth anything at all if this book is successful. What if it's a flop? What if what I say actually doesn't matter at all? The fears are real, people.

"You will always be more than this project or any project. This project will be a powerful gift in and through your life. I think it will kick start a lot of your future. But always know... you are SO AMAZING and SO LOVED. And you are so much more than any calling you have. You are amazing and such an inspiration in the way you are saying yes to this call God has put in your heart. But you are more. Always. I am so excited for all God has in store in this book. But I am more excited about who He is making you to be, and all the work

He is up to in filling you with His love and life. That's why this book is so awesome. Because YOU are. Not the other way around."

In the middle of this semi-mental breakdown I was having without telling anyone about it, one of the friends, Meg, who I let read my draft sent me this text. These words hit hard. They left me crying alone in a coffee shop, which I wish I could say was the first, time but nope. She's the friend that calls me when I need her, without her knowing it. She's the friend who I actually didn't even get the chance to know until after I left California, but her heart is so like Jesus that she loved me better than most people could anyway. There's a lot of lessons in this book from her actually, so Meg, thank you. Thank you for being my friend. God bless you, Meg.

Those words that she sent me, I don't think they're just for me. I think they're for you too. So if there's something that you're pursuing with all of your heart, something that you know in the depths of your soul that you were created for, you're still loved without it. Whatever you do is amazing because YOU are amazing, not the other way around. Don't forget that.

So go write that book. Go sing that song. Go solve those math problems. Do what you're created to do, just don't forget that you're loved either way. And don't forget that if you judge a fish by its ability to climb a tree that fish is going to feel pretty stupid. Thanks, Albert Einstein.

"And once you live a good story, you get a taste for a kind of meaning in life, and you can't go back to being normal; you can't go back to meaningless scenes stitched together by the forgettable thread of wasted time."

– Donald Miller

I used to be quite the stoner. That might be a surprise, might not, but I was and I was just telling my friend Eva about this last night sitting in her car in the parking lot at Mcdonald's. We were in the not so fancy part of Nashville, so in between double checking that our doors were locked and admiring the light up rims on the tires of the cars driving by, I got to tell her a bit of my story, the bit about me being a stoner.

Not a lot of people believe me at first when I tell them this about myself. They look at me, cheesy smile and sometimes over-the-top-niceness and just don't see how it could be a thing. But believe it or not, after smoking my first bowl of weed in a church parking lot, I started to enjoy the hobby a little more than I should. I mean, I was quite the little rebel back in my day. I ditched school and stole my sister's ID to get my bellybutton pierced, tattood a dolphin on my hip, hid a fart machine under my teacher's desk at school, and just tried to party my life away.

I say these things now with some confidence. Like, I'm not pretending it's casual small talk with a cashier at Target or anything like that, but I used to hesitate a bit more before I would share these things. Hesitate enough to not want to put it in a book, at least. Seeing as I became a Christian a bit later in life than most of the friends I surrounded myself with, I was pretty saddened as to why my story couldn't look more like theirs. They grew up in church, went to vacation bible school, all that jazz. I mean, I went to church for a bit as a kid, but as far as my story went, that just wasn't it. I had a past and no, it's not as bad as it could have been, but I was pretty ashamed about it for a good portion of last year. What changed, you ask? Why am I now all of a sudden able to own it on the internet? Well, I realized that my story matters. No, I don't think God actively makes bad things happen. I don't think he put me through hard times because he just felt like it. I think I am who I am and I made the decisions that I made, and God made something beautiful out of it. Now my story gets to impact people who have been through things that never would have been affected if I grew up in church. My story sets those people free, just like a pastor's kid's story can set people with that kind of history as well.

I'm writing in a coffee shop called Portland Brew today. Interestingly enough I don't even like this coffee shop, I was just told recently that Donald Miller comes here a lot so I figured I would push my chances of having another incredible elevator talk with him a little higher. Also, the idea of running into Donald Miller while I'm writing a book inspired by him is really exciting to me.

I think my favorite thing about living in Nashville is the coffee shops. Not because they're trendy or hip or "aesthetically pleasing," as some say, but because of the people in them. Coffee shops in Nashville have a special kind of passion filled crowd. There's the Belmont scholar studying her brains out at the table next to me, glasses resting on the brim of her nose, coffee stains on notebooks from the late night study session she practically just woke up from. Then there's the aspiring audio engineer at the bar top, headphones bigger than his head, putting down his second latte. Then the writers, and there are lots, filling up the couches and stools with their laptops and racing imaginations. Who knows what will come from this coffee shop. Who knows who the future best selling record artist I'm sitting next to is. This coffee shop could very likely be the current home for the future of entertainment. It's crazy. My once again empty cappuccino mug should be ever so honored to sit on the same table as these peoples.

Passion is an interesting thing, and Nashville is filled with it. Similar to what I found to be true in LA, everyone here has a story. Every one is from somewhere, burdened with a dream that needed to be lived, and Nashville is their destination of choice. It's pretty cool to live here amongst that, I think it's why I prefer to write in coffee shops rather than in my own home. It's inspiring to me to chase my dream next to people chasing theirs.

The first thing people typically ask me when I tell them that I'm from Colorado is if I ski or snowboard. Like its this big deal or something, almost like asking if I'm a Backstreet Boys or Nsync kind of woman. Not that it's relevant at the moment, but I'm neither. I was just a straight up Lizzie McGuire kind of kid. Anyway, my answer to the snowboard/ski question is always a big disappointing nah. I tried snowboarding one time, and one time only. That day consisted of getting up, and falling. And getting up, and falling again. Literally for five hours straight I just fell. I fell on my butt, back, hands, neck, face, side, you name it and I guarantee you I fell on it at some point during that day. That was just the bunny slopes though, which I didn't even know were the bunny slopes until we left them for the actual mountain. I thought that was it! But nope. After my first semi-successful trip down the bunny slope I was pushed to move on to the next level. I couldn't feel my body. I promise you this moment was a lot more dramatic than I'm making it sound, even though I know I'm making it very dramatic as it is. I stared that mountain down, held my breath, and realized that there was literally no turning back now. Literally, it just was not possible. Unless for some reason snowboarding uphill suddenly became a thing after I finished this book, just know that at this point in time it was not. That's when the real falling began, and it got so bad that the ski instructor had to come tell me to walk down the rest of the mountain because he was scared I was going to hurt myself. Yeah, it was that bad. So there I was, snowboard under my arm, legs wobbly, tears and snot everywhere imaginable (sorry for the TMI, I just wanted to paint a pretty picture for you). I walked down that mountain like it was my own personal runway on the worst walk of shame of my life. Did that even make sense? Whatever, just know that it was bad and I was quite the hot mess. Not to mention, on the way home I got in a car accident, then had to go straight to work. All in the same day people, all in the same day.

My parents were weirdly amused by my pain, seeing as to how much I ignored them when they told me it wasn't going to be as easy as I thought. Similar to when I ignored them when they told me to dress warm for my first concert at Red Rocks in May. I scoffed as I headed out the door in my shorts and flip flops. That's a whole other story, but it's very important for you to know that the night ended up with me breaking my flip flops, walking barefoot in the mud and snow, borrowing an old man's fishing pants, stranded and a little lost somewhere in Morrison Colorado. I called my mom to pick me up and she said no. I don't blame her. I probably should start listening to my mom.

Some days I feel very artsy and very *Nashville* with my ripped up jeans and top knot bun. There are even days when both my socks match and I really feel like I have my life in order. Then there are some days when I feel more like the version of myself walking around barefoot in the snow with a stranger's fishing pants. Also known as an absolute hot mess. That's what I felt this morning when I strolled in around 8 in the morning. It's not normally like me to stay out all night, maybe it's a little more like Rebel Jackie, but current Jackie doesn't do that too much. No people, this was not one of *those* types of walk of shame mornings, I just felt ridiculous to say the least. The whole night all I wanted to do was run. I wanted to pack up my car and drive to Florida, or some place that wasn't Nashville, at least. Florida just always seems like a good idea especially because there are dolphins there. I don't know how to explain it, I just all of a sudden started having this inner panic attack and wanted to run for the hills. The worst part about it was that there really wasn't any reason for it. I've been in bad situations when wanting to run away is a whole lot more understandable, but last night, life in itself just seemed hard and no matter how much I knew I would regret it, all I could think about doing was running.

I was journaling this morning after my night of feeling insane, and I just put it all out there. I realized that I honestly have no idea what I'm doing. Like sometimes I want to eat ice cream all day, and I just want that to be okay. I have this friend Meagan who's writing a blog. Meagan inspires the hell out of me. Yes, I just said hell. Meagan has a blog called *The Graceful Attempt*, and it's all about embracing our quirks and finding out that there's grace for every ounce of our being. It's about learning how Jesus loves us and that, as she said in her first amazing blog post, "My life is not lived on a pure, white background with a perfectly aligned succulent and beautifully lacquered nails. My life does not always reflect adorable footwear paired with a cold brew held over matching street sign. I do not go romping on the reg through fields of daisies, and I certainly do not faux laugh under a tree of falling cherry blossoms," and that is absolutely okay. Honestly, I don't think anyone's life is actually how it looks on their perfectly filtered Instagram page of succulents and white coffee mugs. It would take too much work, and it would most likely not be that much fun. Anyway, my favorite thing about Meagan is that she's probably just as quirky as me, and she's not pretending to be any other way. I mean her blog post has a picture of her sitting on her bed covered in Doritos, Oreos, and Lays potato chips. Meagan makes me feel like it's okay to be normal. It's okay to have that day that I feel like a hot mess. In my graceful attempt at life, as she says, I'm loved. God bless you, Meagan.

After journaling for so long my overly hot coffee became too cold to drink (I totally drank it anyway), I realized how much I actually liked being a hot mess. I actually really liked the fact that my mismatched socks represent my brain, my Dodger shirt had permanent coffee stains on it from three years ago, and I had no idea how I was going to resist buying every flavor of Girl Scout Cookie cereal out there. I liked it because it just showed how much I need Jesus. My life is a walking, breathing example of how humanity is the epitome of hopeless on its own. But that's okay! Because there's this guy Jesus. I don't know you. I don't know how you feel about Jesus or God, or Christianity in general. Maybe you've been burned by a church, maybe you go to church regularly, maybe Christianity in general is just nonsense to you. Well let me tell you what, that's okay. I love you. If you don't want to follow Jesus, that's fine. You're just going to have to find another absolutely perfect, flawless, all-loving, all-graceful being to follow. It might be a hard thing to come across.

What I'm trying to say is that Jesus is there, he's real, and he's perfect so that we don't have to be. He conquered life, and I'm sure he was the guy whose socks tended to match. His perfection isn't meant to shame us by any means, it's meant to be for us. Like I've said countless times, we're human. Mistakes are inevitable. Feeling like a hot mess, no matter how perfect you make your eyeliner look, is inevitable too. But guess what? Jesus loves us in that mess. That mess can not be messier enough to change that. That's why no matter how "rock-bottomy" you may feel, it's never actually going to be rock bottom.

As this section comes to a close, I feel like it's my obligation to tell you that I spent this whole day at Portland Brew, and no, Donald

Miller did not show up. It's fine, I'm sure he's off writing books that will change my life somewhere else. Maybe next time. I'll keep you posted.

Redemption

*"God was no longer a slot machine but something of a Spirit
that had the power to move men's souls. I seemed to have been
provided answers to questions that i had yet to ask, questions
that God sensed or had even instilled in the lower reaches of my
soul. The experience of becoming a Christian was delightful."*

– Donald Miller

BEFORE LAST WEEKEND, I CAN HONESTLY SAY
that I had no idea how to go to a wedding. Am I supposed to bring
presents? Food? My own fork? What kind of dress do I wear? My
old homecoming dress is available and tempting, or should I go
with the princess style prom dress I was handed down from Alex?
The thoughts were endless. The this-or-that questions were a little
over the top and I felt like a helpless kid who needed a mom, so I
called mine.

I was invited to the wedding of a very dear friend of mine
last weekend and I was honored, but mentally extremely unprepared
mentally. I didn't buy my dress or even find the registry until the day
of, and didn't even know the address to where I was going until right
before I figured I should start the drive. I'm telling you; Hot. Mess.

Best way to describe me. I probably yelled at my mom on the phone the whole time I was trying to figure this stuff out, as well. At least she found it endearing.

My panic-stricken self finally got it together, stuffed my face with the typical Jackie G style comfort food featuring half a jar of peanut butter slapped onto one banana, and I hit the road. The thing that I have yet to mention about this wedding, however, was that it was going to be the first time I would see a bunch of my friends from the ministry school I went to since I dropped out. It was the first time I would see them, see the old teachers, pastors, all of them. So yes, I had more nerves than just whether or not my shoes were the right combination of dressy and casual for an outdoor back porch style wedding.

Ever since I had left the school, there was something that shifted in my heart regarding church. Like I've mentioned before about my thoughts on living in the Bible Belt, it has left me with a quite a bit of church baggage that I didn't have before. Suddenly the typical conversations about Jesus that I would have with people on a daily basis just didn't flow like they used to. There was a wall up between me and the church world out here, and I just didn't want to be a part of it, as much as I thought I was going to want to. I didn't want to have the conversations about Jesus with people because I didn't want to blend into the typical Nashville church crowd. It seemed fake and I felt flat out bitter. But do you want to know what I hate? Yeah, being bitter. Bitterness is the worst because no matter how much I didn't want to be I just could not seem to get over it. I would do my best to get over it, but it felt like a parasite that I couldn't get out of my system. I felt annoying talking about it because it had been a bit of time since everything went down, but the hurt was still there and I couldn't get it out of my head. So, there it sat.

It all really seemed to hit me when my friend Eppic was in town visiting me from LA. Epps knew me very, very well during my period in LA. He saw both the ups and downs, but more than anything he saw the passion and fire that I used to have in conversations about Jesus. Nothing held me back during that time in my life. I was all-in and I didn't care who knew. I read my Bible every spare minute I had, no matter where I was or who I was with. If someone even vaguely mentioned Jesus my ears would perk up like a dog when the doorbell rings. Epps and I used to live only two buildings apart, actually, so we would have Bible studies at the park across the street every morning where we would go through different books and ask each other questions. It really was a beautiful thing because we were both hungry and both just looking for God to speak through something in our time together. That was definitely my favorite part of my day back then and everybody knew it.

So Eppic was in town visiting and I hadn't seen him in quite some time. I was driving him around, playing tour guide, showing all my favorite juice bars and coffee shops when I was trying to explain to him where my newfound church baggage came from. Honestly, I was embarrassed. I didn't care talking about it with newer friends that I had in Nashville, but Eppic knew the real me. Eppic saw the passionate Jackie on fire and excited for any and all things church like, and I could tell that he knew something was off. But then again, maybe he didn't. Either way, I sure knew and I so deeply feared that he knew it as well.

"So when did you seem to get back to normal?"

Epps asked me that question and I had no idea what to tell him.

"Uhhhh… There wasn't really a big moment. I guess it has been more of a process? I'm not sure."

We didn't talk about it much more after that, but oh, I sure thought about it. I don't think I

stopped thinking about it since, actually. I wanted my moment, I wanted my old self back but I didn't know how I was supposed to get there.

There I was, in my blue lace dress and lips hopefully in the right shade of red lipstick. The ceremony ended and I was sitting in near view of the cupcake table when something shifted in my heart at this wedding. I don't know if it was just because weddings are beautiful and this one specifically meant a lot to me because of who my friend was, but something deeper happened that night. Spending time with the people from my old school at this wedding somehow began to peel away at the hurt that I had felt from before. It took a minute for me to stop obsessing in my head over the idea that all they saw was "the girl who dropped out of ministry school" plastered over my forehead, but the second that fear went away, the second I was able to breathe. I finally stopped rambling about every possible subject I could think of in order to avoid the big, "where did you go?" question, finally stopped asking each and every question in the book to keep people talking to avoid a potential awkward silence, and I just breathed. I watched my friends dance, smile, giggle, and just be. Peace was in the air. There was more than just a wedding that day, there was a newness. It felt light, and I liked it.

It was at that moment that I realized that I didn't have to find the moment that put me back to normal. I didn't need someone to knock the sense into me so I can find the old Jackie again. The truth was that I wasn't the same, but that is what's normal. There's this thing called life, and in life there's this thing called growth. At that moment, I began to get rid of the idea that I needed to get back to the way I was, and start looking forward to who I was becoming. No, that same innocence that I used to feel regarding church wasn't there like it had been in the past. But at this wedding, I got to experience the bitterness of what I had felt lift off, and I got to step into the newness of where I was headed. There's this problem in my head sometimes where I look to the past a lot. Maybe it's because I'm a writer, maybe I'm just an avid reflector, who knows. But I look back at past seasons and tend to want the old back. I disregard the progress or growth I've made, or anything negative about past seasons and just want to go back because it's comfortable. We go back to what we know because we've already been there. There's no surprises, we know what to expect, and it's familiar. It's the reason why people are scared to move away from their hometowns or quit their jobs. It's why we sometimes get stuck in bad relationships or run back to ex-boyfriends. The future is unknown, and I hate to admit it but it scares me. When I'm uncomfortable with where I'm at, I look back and want to run. It's why lately I've wanted to run and hide out at my parents house in Colorado and play Wii Sports in the basement. Since things got uncomfortable in my feelings towards church, I was desperate to get back to the Old Church Jackie when what I should have been doing was looking forward to who I was becoming because of the experiences that I had. I wasn't just bitter at my school because it gave me a weird experience, I was bitter at my school because I felt like it robbed me of myself. I felt like it stole my innocence and now there was nothing I could do to get it back. I saw myself as the victim. Truth is, that school did not do any of those things to me. That school and the people that were a part of it were being who they were and living true to their convictions, and at that wedding I was finally able to see it.

I'm done chasing after the old versions of myself. People grow for a reason. Change happens, and it's about time I stop being scared of it and embrace the goodness that it can bring. It's our experiences that shape us and mold us into who we're created to become. I'm never going to be the old Jackie G in Burbank, but I will always be Jackie G. I'm not sure exactly what that means, but what I do know is that church is no longer a sore subject for me. That means a lot of things, but it does not mean that I'm an old version of myself. It does mean that I'm a new version, I'm going to actively be bold about my relationship with Jesus, and it's going to feel new every single day. For that, I am thankful.

~

I find it absolutely hilarious that I have ever worked in the music industry. Besides the short period in my life where I was planning to start a band in my basement and make Alex sing with me like Aly and AJ, it was never anything that I seriously wanted to do with my life. Yes, I am very capable of playing one song and one song only on a guitar, and I did in fact teach myself Mary Had a Little Lamb on the recorder once, but when it comes to the music business as a whole I really didn't see myself being a part of it. That being said, when I was done being a personal assistant, I thought I was done. No more tours, no more music videos, I was going to be strictly a music admirer from here on out.

Another thing I find really interesting is how Jesus seems to like to bring things around full circle more times than could be considered a coincidence. I'm not sure if he does that in your life, but it's really common in mine. Similar to what he did at the wedding with my friends from school, he seems to like to bring me back into situations that ended in a not-so-good way and shed a new light on it. It's almost like redemption is a big deal to him. Something like that.

Remember that friend I was telling you about earlier who showed me what the genuine love of Jesus looked like for the first time in my life when I was desperate for it? The one who I was on tour with during my year of shame and showed me the most unconditional love I had ever seen in my life? Well, she was back in Nashville visiting for a bit when I was asked to join her and her band for a tour they were about to leave for in Florida. Thinking that my tour life was over a long time ago, I was a little caught off guard by both the offer and my sudden desire to go, and had absolutely no reason to say no. I was only free Wednesdays through Sundays, and that's when they needed me. Coincidence? Never. Next thing I know I'm packing my bags, grabbing an Uber, and hopping on a plane that would take me to another adventure of life on the road. I was excited, but to be real with you I was more nervous than I knew. The last time I was on a tour bus, I was a complete polar opposite version of myself. The last time I laid in a closed off bunk and stared at the ceiling of a bus, the thoughts that went through my head were just not so pretty. I hated myself. I didn't know Jesus, I was waking up smothered in regrets and shame and I just hid. That was my life, and revisiting it didn't sound appealing.

There were going to be some familiar faces on this tour as well. Besides my dear friend, we were also being joined by a few other members from the old tour crew on this run and I was getting ready to face them. The last time they saw me I was most likely either drunk or planning my next time to get there. Would they believe that I was a new person? Were they going to assume the worst? Was I going to give into peer pressure to go back to the old ways? So many thoughts went through my head on the plane ride there, and they were all sounding a lot like those and I was not much of a fan.

I arrived in Florida and pulled up to the rehearsal space where the band was camped out. The tour bus looked the exact same as I remembered, and I dropped my stuff off in the same bunk. It was like I never left. The last time I laid in that bunk was the first time I actually wanted to die. I hate writing those words but they're true and the last thing I wanted was to relive them, but somehow I knew that I was exactly where I needed to be.

You know what happened? The day went on, I hung out with people that I loved, heard some killer music, and that night I put my head down on my pillow and I stared at the ceiling the same way I did two years prior. However, this time as I laid there, I got to be told by Jesus how much he loved me. This time the thoughts that went through my head sounded a lot like value and peace, and a lot less like shame and self-hatred. They were whispers of belonging and purpose. I laid there and soaked up the worship music through my headphones and felt at peace. I laid there and sat in the truth that I am his daughter, and I am loved. Compared to two years ago when

I just laid there and wanted to not exist, I was speechless. Suddenly, the past stopped mattering so much. It stopped having as much of a say in who I was today. The memories of the bad began to become replaced by the new memories of where my life was at right now. That's when I realized that creating an opportunity to go back on tour where my problems originally began, was the kindest thing in the world that God could have done for me in that moment. The old is gone. It's just not real anymore, and it's not who I am nor will it ever be again.

There was a night on this tour when I was invited to go out to dinner with the band by my friend's Dad. They called it family dinner, and honestly being invited was extremely unexpected. When I was in the old days of being an assistant, I was trained to have the "artist in the front" mentality, so the idea of being included in something with the musicians was new and special. We went to this dinner, and it was by far the fanciest restaurant I had ever been to. It was probably the greatest tasting food I had ever eaten, and it just kept coming. Course after course, hour after hour, I felt like I was a part of something. I looked around me and noticed that it wasn't just me who received an invitation outside the band; everyone did. The bus driver, the roadies, everyone was included at the table. Something special was happening.

After the dinner I felt like I couldn't thank her dad enough. I didn't feel worthy of being there, worthy of food as good as that food tasted, if I'm being real, but when I thanked him all he could say was, "thank YOU!" He thanked me for being there. WHAT? He thanked ME. That blew my mind and made absolutely no sense at all.

I think that a dinner in Heaven with Jesus would look a lot like that one did that night. We would all be gathered around the table, unlimited supplies of incredible food, conversation, the best chocolate chip cookies in the world, and a feeling of belonging in the air that isn't capable of being described by mere words on a page. Feeling unworthy in a scenario like that would make plenty of sense, but going to Jesus to give gratitude, I wouldn't be anything less than surprised if his response was that as well. I think Jesus would look at us and tell us how happy he was that we were there, how much he loved being around us, and how he would never want Heaven any other way. There's a line in a song by Hillsong that reminds me of this that says, "He didn't want heaven without us." Every single time I hear those words in that song, something in my heart comes alive. Jesus starts to make both more sense and less sense at the same time. I get similar feels when I read the part in the Bible at the end of John when Jesus just finished dying for everyone, came back to life, and decided to make his disciples breakfast. Think about how that would feel to be one of the disciples that day, coming in from fishing to find the man who just stood in the place for you and took the most insane death possible by man so that you could be saved, just casually whipping up some eggs and bacon for you. How unworthy do you think that would make you feel? That's my Jesus right there.

⁓

I really like the idea of God replacing the bad memories in our lives. I think he does it on purpose and I think he loves every bit of it. I have felt more healing in my heart from situations like this than I thought would ever be possible. I found out that in these moments, Jesus doesn't just put things back to normal when they break, he makes them a million times better instead. He doesn't put it back, he pulls it forward. I think that's what redemption means, and I'm learning to expect that in more things than not. I'm actually learning to expect Jesus to show up in greater ways in pretty much every area of my life, and let me tell you, it has been quite the show. Again, that might sounds naive, but I'm starting to learn that being naive isn't always bad. If being naive means expecting Jesus to show up in miraculous ways every single day, then there is nothing that I'd rather be.

This happened to me around the time I first moved to Nashville. I had just moved into my second apartment since I got here, and the only way I feel like I can describe my life is messy. I was driving through this area of Nashville called West End for the first time since I got there, and looking around I quickly began to recognize where I was.

A couple years prior, I was in Nashville for a business trip during my personal assistant days. Right after we got off the tour, we headed for what I thought seemed like the greatest city in the world. I knew absolutely nothing about Nashville back then, but whenever I heard about it I knew I needed to go. So after getting told we would be headed there for couple weeks I grabbed my cowboy boots, teased my blonde poofy hair, and packed my bags, ready to hit the road.

During my time in Nashville with my boss, a lot happened. In a nutshell, I did some pretty stupid stuff including locking my keys in my car not once, but twice. Not two separate times, but two times in a row. The AAA guy got there to get them out the first time, then

I had to flag him down as he was driving away to come get them out again because, within 20 seconds of him leaving I managed to somehow lock them in again. I did my fake blonde hair justice that day.

That's not the worst thing that happened to me out there, unfortunately. Right as we got there the first night, we stopped by the Ed Sheeran show at the Bridgestone, then went straight to Broadway. I had a fake ID and I was very prepared to use it. I just went back to watch my old vlogs from my time in Nashville, and the main thing I notice from myself at the time was that I just looked empty. I was searching for something, anything, to feel loved and important and if I was going to find that bar hopping with a guy, so be it. There we went, from one bar to the next, one drink to the next, and one mistake to the next.

After casually hopping around to see different cover bands perform the same playlist over and over again with an extra addition of *Don't Stop Believing* to top off the night, we would head back to the Airbnb. That's when the mistakes took place and the shame continued to pile on. Morning after morning, I would wake up miserable. It wasn't just the hangover, it was the emotional turmoil to top it off. There were a few of these mornings where I was encouraged to go buy the Plan B pill for myself, because this could be a way for me to "learn my lesson." Yes, this was a pretty low point in my life. I would put sunglasses on to hide behind, ear buds in my ears to tune out whatever noise there was, and tried to drown out any sort of emotion that might pop up. One morning I would walk into Walgreens and ask the lady in the pharmacy the dreaded question, pay the $49.99, and be on my way. The next morning I would walk into a Ritaid to do the same thing all over again. This would continue, and each morning I would find a new spot to go in because the last thing I would want to do is go to the same place twice. Just the thought of facing the same lady at the pharmacy more than one time with this question sounded like the worst thing in the world, whether I was feeling my emotions or not.

Flashing forward again to when I moved here last year and was driving through West End, I passed by the different pharmacies that I ran through back then. Once I realized where I was, everything became familiar. After I recognized the pharmacies, I started to recognize the hotels and the bars, then the restaurants. They were all the places that made up those few weeks of my life a couple years back, and I felt like I wanted to throw up. I wanted to pull over, get out of my car, and be sick. I was also pissed off, for a lack of better words. I was angry because the shame from a few years ago came back, and dealing with that in the middle of the current problems in my life was not exactly ideal. I hated that this place was tainted with that part of my story. I hated that my new home had marks of my old life over it that I wanted to be erased.

I went to a worship service that night that I actually didn't want to go to, like, at all. Normally I enjoyed them, but after remembering who I used to be on my fun little drive that day, the last thing I wanted to do was bring that before God in a worship service. I knew the truths about God loving me either way, no matter what, etc., but I didn't feel those truths in my heart. There's a pretty big difference between head knowledge and heart knowledge.

There have been different occasions in the past two years of knowing Jesus where he would show me pictures in my mind during worship and prayer times. It was rare, and each time was absolutely life changing. At this worship service that I felt dragged to at the time, I closed my eyes and just sat there. In all honesty, I was pretending to be into it, counting down how much longer I thought there was in the back of my head until it was over. But once I took a deep breath and stopped thinking for five seconds, a picture came into my head of myself on West End two years ago, running into the pharmacies. However this time, I wasn't alone. Jesus was with me when I was walking into Walgreens and regardless of how ashamed I was, he didn't look anything less than excited. He wasn't just excited, he was stoked, and it made the least bit of sense in the world. The Jackie from two years ago didn't see him, but he was still there.

I was really confused by this image while I was at the worship service. It was annoying because I couldn't for the life of me figure out what it meant, and the idea of Jesus being really excited while I was really ashamed seemed ridiculous and way out of character from everything I knew about him.

I left the worship service and drove home in complete silence. I didn't turn on the radio, didn't call anyone on the phone, I just listened the engine of my car, which I don't do very often. I got home, threw myself face down on my bed without even having my nightly bowl of cereal and begged Jesus to tell me what the heck was going on. That's when I heard him loud and clear. Jesus wasn't mad, he wasn't sad, he wasn't anything but toe-tapping excited because during the days when I was running to get Plan B pills, I was so close to knowing him. These Plan B pill days all happened in September of 2014, and it was October of 2014 when I came face to face with my Jesus. I was literally one month from that and I didn't even know it. All I knew was how ashamed and disgusting I felt and how many stupid mistakes I couldn't stop making, but Jesus didn't care. Jesus saw me and he loved me anyway. Despite the disgusting truth behind what I was doing, all he could see was that my time to meet him was getting so close, and he couldn't be any more thrilled. Only from the purest form of love can something like that happen. Only from the purest form of love can something like that heal someone's heart in such a beautiful, indescribable way. I woke up the next morning and couldn't feel more peaceful. God is a redeemer. He heals things layer by layer, moment by moment in a time frame that only he really knows about.

Oh. My. Gosh. During a time in my life that I thought condemned me, Jesus didn't even care, he just wanted to know me, and he wanted me to know him. He wanted me to come home.

There was a story I was told while I was involved in that ministry, Christ Life, a couple years back. It was a story that this reminded me of, and one that will forever change the way that I view God. There was a girl who was kidnapped at a very young age, and got stuck in some really bad environments. She was used and abused by men, addicted to drugs, alcohol, you name it. She hadn't seen her family since she was a little girl, but day and night her parents were searching everywhere for her. They never gave up. Their whole lives now and forever would revolve around finding their little girl. One day their daughter finally escaped from the life she was trapped in, and was out on the streets trying to find her way when she came across a flyer with her childhood picture on it. With vague memories of the day it was taken, she went to the address listed on the flyer. Stepping up to the front porch, she slowly knocked on the door. After a not so subtle peek through the blinds, her dad pulled the door practically off the hinges to greet his long lost daughter. There was more excitement in his heart than he ever thought was possible, and all he could think about was how much he wanted to hold his little baby girl again.

The thing about this story that really got me was the fact that it was clear as day that after the life the girl had been living, there were going to be a lot of things that needed to be changed. She was addicted to drugs, smoked cigarettes, had an extremely understandable attitude problem, etc. But what gets me is that her dad sees this, but all he can think about is how thankful he was to have her home. Those problems were things that, yes, needed to be changed and worked through as time went on, but the most important thing in the world at the moment she came back was the fact that he had his little girl back.

I could be wrong (even though after reading the story about the prodigal son I highly doubt it), but I think that's how God feels when one of his lost kids finds their way back to him. I don't think it matters in the slightest bit what they've done or what mess they just got themselves in, all that matters is that they're home.

That's where the confusion comes in today's Christian culture, and it really breaks my heart. People think they have to pull themselves together, get all their crap in order before they can go to God. I had a friend once who told me that if she stepped into a church, she would burn the place down. That comment alone shows just how wrong we've represented what church is meant to be, and sadly, who Jesus is. I mean, I get it. I've been there. I've felt like I wasn't good enough to be around God. But the scary truth about it is that I never will be. That's the scary truth, but also the beauty behind it.

Seeing Jesus next to me, excited beyond belief during a time that I would have never in a million years chosen for Jesus to see, changed my life. He wasn't concerned about what made me broken or mad at where I had gone wrong, which was a lot of areas if I do say so myself, he was just so unbelievably excited to soon hold me in his arms and bring me home. That right there, that's the real heart of Jesus.

"Welcome to the real world. It sucks. You're gonna love it!"

– Monica Geller

Okay, so this is the time in the story where I'm about to tell you something really embarrassing. Like come on you guys, I've shared a lot of stories with you all in this book so I almost feel like what do I have to lose, you know? What's left to be embarrassed about? But you know too much already that it doesn't make sense not to share this story with you as well. But here's the thing, if you're a guy, do yourself a favor and don't read this section. I'm giving you an out here. This is an opportunity for you to save yourself some confusion and embarrassment for yourself, so you should probably take it. I didn't have to warn you, but I feel as though I should so I am.

For those of you who listened to me and skipped/are about to skip, bravo. I congratulate you for being gentlemanly enough to make that choice. For those of you who stayed, have fun. I figured not everybody was going to listen anyway. But Dad, if specifically you are still reading this section, I know you well enough to know that you don't want to read this section, so please, just trust me and skip ahead. Love you. Okay here it goes, you've been warned, no complaining past this point.

So I work at a job where we are forced against our will to wear white pants. Yes, you all see where I'm going with this now. We wear bright white pants that we are told to keep as clean as we can, and last weekend I had a shift at work where that just wasn't happening. For the first five months of me living in Nashville, there was so much change and emotional confusion that my period took it upon itself to take a little break. Not that I was sad about not having a period for five months, but it was just weird. No, I did not think I was pregnant, but yes, people asked me to double check regularly. Since my period took five months off, I stopped being consistently prepared every week. I tell you this because it makes me feel better about what happened to me at work last week.

It was the beginning of the shift in my very, very busy restaurant when my worst fear was realized. Already an emotional wreck due to the unfortunate amount of hormones that came with the curse us women deal with every single month, I went to the bathroom to discover that yes, I had indeed bled through my white pants. It wasn't even just a little bit, it was a lot. It wasn't even just on the butt, it had somehow managed to make its way down to the side of my pant leg. How? Not sure. Not really worried about it, but I was definitely worried about what I was about to do.

After a five-minute panic session and urgent SOS text messages I was sending to everyone I could possibly think of that would understand my dilemma, I took a sad, sad stroll back out to my section. Head dragging in shame, back against the wall as much as possible, I was having middle school flashbacks like crazy. I felt like a 12-year-old girl, it was *bad*. So what was the first instinct I had? Obviously to tell every person I could before they saw themselves, because I had no doubt in my mind that they would. The first couple people I filled in were pretty cool about it, they made me feel like it wasn't THAT noticeable so I walked out to check on my tables with a bit more confidence than I had before. Not to mention they were all pretty close together, and at exact eye level to my butt so every time I would turn around to chat up the table nearby, they had a front row seat to my middle school trauma flashback.

The stains being "not that bad" felt too good to be true and if I was going to be confident, I at least wanted to be sure it wasn't a lie, so I casually made my way to the other side of the restaurant where my friend's section was and filled her in on my nightmare. That's where before I knew it, everyone and their mom found out about what was going on, and the truth started to spill out about how bad it actually was. So who did they decide to tell? That's right, my manager. My manager was a dude. He looked down at me, absolutely uncomfortable as can be, said, "I don't see anything, you're fine." Then scoffed at me and walked away. NO DUH he didn't see anything, he was looking at me from the front where I had an apron on. No way did he have any idea what kind of inner turmoil I was feeling.

If my day wasn't bad enough, about five minutes later I walked into the kitchen to check on the multiple food tickets that were at almost an hour wait time for some reason, a different one of my managers, one that I believe truly does hate me for some reason, turned and screamed at me for being there for about 30 seconds.

Everyone was there, everyone saw it happen, and I turned and ran outside so that I wouldn't be seen crying next to any tacos.

After being told by pretty much every single girl employee there that they would have straight up walked out if it was them with the stains on their pants, I stuck it out. I don't really know why I did it, it's not like selling tacos is my die hard passion that I couldn't even stand the thought of missing out on it that day, regardless of the girl stains. I don't know, maybe I stuck it out because I didn't want to get fired, maybe I did it because I was scared of my managers. Or maybe, just maybe I did it for the same reason I stayed in the game each time I got a concussion in softball. I got a lot of concussions. The best one was when I got hit, then smiled and asked if my hair was okay.

I have a few reasons behind telling you this extremely embarrassing story about myself. One is that I'm learning that there's going to be a lot of times in life where we have to do things that we don't want to do. There's going to be plenty part-time jobs with mean bosses that we're going to have to work, plenty of tables we're going to have to bus, floors we have to sweep, trays we're going to have to dry and then re-dry because we didn't dry them good enough the first time, and so on. Sometimes life just doesn't go from high school to college to your dream job. Sometimes we have to pay a lot of money for taxes, and sometimes we have to live in an apartment where there's an occasional cockroach or two, or three, or too many to be okay so we end up sleeping in our cars. Yes, that happened to me and no, I don't want to talk about it. This might actually be the most logical, realistic part of my book now that I think about it. I'm not generally a very realistic person. I've been called "the dreamer" on way more than just one occasion, so for me to write things like this is a little funny. But it's true. Whether or not we're working our dream job, we still have to work hard. Whether we're a bathroom attendant cleaning toilets and handing people paper towels after they wash their hands, or we're famous pop stars touring the world, it shouldn't make a difference how hard we work. It's ironic because I'm telling you this as I'm dreading going to my waitress job in a couple hours and the idea of drying trays and selling tacos to the very best of my ability sounds like the least fun thing ever. I'm not trying to say that I'm good at this whole work-hard-no-matter-what thing, but I'm trying. I think we should all try a little harder at that, because every job we have here has a purpose behind it.

One of my biggest pet peeves is when people feel entitled to the big fancy jobs where they sing songs on stage or make important decisions about data and fonts and stuff. They think they're too good to sell tacos, and because they feel so entitled, they complain while they're doing it and do an absolutely terrible job. Then they just end up bitter. I'm saying "they," but in all honesty, I've totally been that person before. I think a lot of people have, and all I'm saying right now is that I want to be better at that. I truly believe that the bathroom attendant's job is just as important as the movie star who's using the fancy bathroom the attendant is working at. There's a reason Jesus says the least is the greatest in the Kingdom. That wasn't meant to just be ironic and thought provoking, it's actually a practical thing that a lot of us don't understand. We get so caught up in our "calling," each one of us thinking that our calling is to be rich and famous. What if your calling was to serve people? What if your calling was to love people where you're at, which right now may be selling tacos or cleaning bathrooms? It's just a thought, I guess. All that to say, I'm thankful for my job selling tacos and drying trays.

My only other real reason for telling you that story is honestly to get you to laugh. I realize that a lot of the stories I've been sharing in this book have been a little more on the intense side emotionally, and I think it's really important to have some humor in the midst of that. Not to fake a smile, not to use humor as a defense mechanism or anything crazy like that. I want to add humor to my story simply because that's just part of who I am. I like to laugh, I like to smile, and I like to make fun of myself, and I think that's perfectly fine. I've been called a robot for doing things like this, and yes, I'm aware that putting a smile on when things are hard can be bad at times, but I'm also aware that who I am is beautiful and I don't think I have to change all that about myself. So I'm sorry to offend anyone, but in the middle of the drama, I'm going to tell you some jokes. No, you don't have to laugh, but I'm going to keep being me. So go ahead, I give you permission to laugh at me as much as you want here. After all, it really was embarrassing.

grace

"It seemed too good to be true. That's grace."

– Judah Smith

I'VE BEEN NOTICING THIS NEW PATTERN develop in my life where Jesus has been giving me closure in a lot of areas that have needed it pretty desperately. He's been bringing things around full circle and putting periods on the end of sentences that I didn't think would ever get one. What the craziest and coolest thing about that is that I'm coming to the end of writing my book. I've never written a book before, which means I really don't know what it looks like for it to be finished. I'm not sure if it's a feeling, a conclusion, a word count, who knows. So I have been trying to think of how I wanted to tie it all up, what I want to say, when all of a sudden the ending to this part of my story pretty much started developing right before my eyes. I'm experiencing the ending of this story right now. I'm living it current day, I just have to find the words to write it out as if I was a reporter or something. It's just fun because I don't think I'm writing it. I think Jesus is writing it, and I can't wait to see how it ends. I get to be at peace with where I'm at, live in the tension of the unanswered questions, unsolved problems, and know that the ending is already planned out.

I ran into an old friend last week. This was someone that I actually thought I might never see again. It was a person who used to be a ginormous and incredible part of my life, yet also someone who has unfortunately been a part of the greatest heartache for me and people that I love. I hadn't seen this friend for over a year, and after running into him for the third time in a month, in two different cities on separate sides of the country, this felt like more of a coincidence.

When I had first moved to Nashville a year ago, which if I'm being real, was an attempt to run away from this person and the pain that happened, I received a phone call. This call was informing me that this person was moving to Nashville as well. Standing behind a coffee shop, same coffee shop as I'm writing in today actually, my body crumbled to the floor and I broke down in tears. I was just angry, there's really no better way of putting it. I wanted my fresh start in Nashville. I wanted no trace of past wounds or mistakes to follow me, and now someone from one of the deepest shame stories of my life was on the way to my new city. I prayed long, and I prayed hard that I wouldn't run into this guy. I was scared of seeing him. I was scared of facing my pain again. Now, Nashville is no LA. It's a pretty small town and people tend to run in similar circles, so the odds weren't exactly in my favor. But I mustered up my faith and I asked Jesus to protect me from running into this person until I would be ready to face him. That day felt unreachable, but like if God can part the Red Sea, he should have no problem keeping my path away from his.

Why was he moving here? If God can control things, why was I so sure that he wanted me to move to Nashville, but now this guy was moving here as well? I was so mad.

"Imagine having no one to fear."

Last week, almost a year later from the day I got that phone call and prayed that prayer, the day had finally come. I was driving my car through Germantown when a strangely familiar face appeared on the sidewalk next to me. There he was. Two times earlier that month I ran into him as well, and it felt like it was time.

I stopped my car, rolled down my window, and just decided to say hello. He asked me to get coffee and, "catch up for like ten minutes," and with all the freedom in the world to say no, I chose to say yes.

That day I sat across the table from a man who I chose to make mistakes with. A man who hurt me. A man who hurt people that I loved. A man who I hurt people that I loved with. A man who was broken. A man who had been hurt. A man who was forgiven. A man who was a human being. A human being who knew Jesus and let that let that change him.

That's when I realized that this man sitting in front of me is actually no different than me. He's broken, I'm broken. He's in desperate need of grace, I'm in desperate need of grace. If you've read any part of this book you'll be well aware of that. But just as I was forgiven for where I went wrong, both with him and every other area of my life, so was he.

That day, sitting face to face with my past, my mistakes, my fears, I got to let it all go. My anger was gone. I had a conversation. I forgave, not just with my words, but with my heart. Let me tell you this, the amount of closure that I received following this conversation was unreal. The amount of peace in my heart was unexplainable. That day in Germantown, I finally was able to forgive my boss, and he forgave me. There was peace, closure, healing, a brand new beginning. The shame was gone.

The thing that was so refreshing about this conversation was that we really owned our stuff. I wasn't a victim, he wasn't a victim, we were both fully capable of making our own decisions, and in the past, there were a lot of decisions that were not so good. But the main thing that was evident in him was his ability to own his stuff. He messed up and he knew it. I messed up and I knew it. There was no one to blame this on, it was time for me to just own it as well. It felt easier to grab onto the victim role in all of this because it made me hate myself less. If I was "manipulated," maybe I wasn't so bad afterall? Maybe it wasn't my fault? I was hiding from what I had done, and in hiding there is never healing. So now as a grown human, I can own my mistakes. I can own where I messed up and make my own choice to both forgive, and receive forgiveness.

The thing about this that blows my mind the most isn't just that I was capable of experiencing forgiveness that felt this powerful, but it's the fact that God is real and God knows me. He was there with me behind that coffee shop a year ago. He saw my tears, heard my cries, and he listened. He didn't just listen, but he cared. He knew me then, and he knows me now after the immense healing journey that he had taken me on throughout the year. It was time this part of my past had a period at the end. Bitterness is poison, and the bitterness I felt before I was able to release this was slowly destroying me. I didn't have to walk away from that conversation feeling shame or guilt like I would have before. The fact that I was able to sit down across the table and feel the peace and grace that I did is actually a massive win. It shows how far the healing journey Jesus has taken me on has gone. It shows that honestly, Jesus is real and grace is the most freeing feeling in the world.

I walked away from that conversation feeling incredibly free, but also incredibly scared. I was scared because this was a person who caused not only me, but people close to me pain. So if I forgave him, what does that mean? If I let go of the bitterness in my heart towards this person who had hurt me, is that hurting everyone else? Am I allowed to stop being angry? Are people going to be mad at me for choosing to get coffee with him? What will people think of me for that? It just exposed a massive load of questions and inse-curities in me that I didn't realize were there. At the end of it all, I got to blatantly see how deeply I feared people, and being scared of people sucks.

My first instinct was to go ask everybody what they thought. "That would fix everything!" I thought to myself. Just do what every-one else says! So I did. I went ahead and called up every "big sister" type figure I could think of. I needed advice and I needed it fast.

That's when I realized a pretty intense truth about myself that I think, deep down, I've always known was there, but now needed to come to terms with.

I make good decisions.

Amy Pape has repeatedly been instilling that into my head for as long as I've known her. Text after text, phone call after phone call, if there's anything she wants me to understand it's that I make good decisions. For the longest time I couldn't get myself to believe her. I thought she was being nice and encouraging, as she always is, but I didn't feel like those words were quite true because I just didn't trust myself. I knew what kind of bad decisions I've made, I knew what people thought of me because of them, so how was it possible for me to do a good job of being responsible for myself in a situation like this? That day I was at a point in my life when I desperately needed to. I realized that if I actually trusted myself, if I actually trusted my own choices, my life would look a lot different than it did.

So you know what? I think I make good decisions. I think I hear Jesus really well and I think I need to start trusting myself more and stop letting so many people tell me what to do and how to feel. I don't think these different people should have as loud of voices in my life as I've given them. I think when it gets down to what really matters, grace and forgiveness and redemption should be at the center of literally everything, no matter what anyone else has to say about it. Every relationship, every decision, every conversation should be centered around that. It's the point of why we're here and why we're okay and I'm absolutely in love with that. So I'm choosing to start trusting myself more because I hear Jesus. There's not one possible way for everyone to be happy with my decisions, everyone to agree, but that's a part of life that it's time I got used to. Every choice has a consequence.

It's absolutely okay and wise to go to trusted leaders and community to get advice, but it stops being okay when those voices become louder in my head than Jesus's voice. It stops being okay when I make it a habit to resort to everyone else's advice in order to stop taking responsibility for my own decisions. From the outside it seems safe to be "confused" or "unsure," but it also just eliminates the opportunity to own my own choices. It steals the chance for me to own my own story by handing off the script to someone else.

I'm not in debt to anyone. I don't owe people my life, my decisions, none of that. It's about time I stepped out from the role of "little sister" and stepped into the role of Jackie G. Alex, my actual big sister, recently told me to "take off those little sister shoes and give them to Goodwill or something." I'm not going to make decisions and then hide them, I'm going to make decisions and own them. If I want to choose grace, I get to choose grace. If I want to choose to eat a chocolate cupcake instead of a salad, I get to eat a damn chocolate cupcake because I'm a grown up and it's just one of the perks. However, making my own choices means having to own my own consequences. That means I have to face the people who disagree without passing the blame off on who I got my advice from, and the potential stomach ache I'll most likely get in the morning from the food choices. That's just life. This just means that I'm responsible for me, Suzy is responsible for Suzy, and Steve is responsible for Steve. It's a little thing called boundaries, and I'm starting to get really good at understanding how they work.

Fear of man is dangerous. I've struggled with a fear of what people will say or think about me for far too long now. Sometimes though, you really do have to just not care what people think. It's getting to the point where I have to choose if I actually believe in Jesus or not. Because, if Jesus is real, if all this stuff about how he tells us to live our lives is true, then why aren't I listening? We're told to forgive everyone who offends us 7x70 times. We're told to not keep records of wrongs, we're told to love our enemies, love our neighbors, turn the other cheek, forgive and expect nothing in return, etc. I get to make the choice to listen to Jesus in that which also means, "hating my mother," "hating my brother," etc. All that Jesus means when he says that, in my opinion, is that they're not my ultimate authority; I don't live to please them, I live to please Jesus. If I make it a choice to forgive, have grace and healing be the center of who I am, then that's my choice. Some people won't be happy with that, and I have to learn to let that be okay. I have to learn to not fear what people might do or think. I make my own decisions, I make GOOD decisions, I just have to start taking responsibility for them. #GodBlessAmyPape.

I'm stepping out from my role of "little sister" from here on out. Of course I still am one, but that being my identity has done so much more harm than good for me. When I put my "little sister" shoes on and let everyone else tell me what to do, I'm putting them on pedestals in my life. I'm letting their voices become louder than God's voice, and that's a terrible place to be. My identity is Jackie G, and I'm really proud of that. I'm not ashamed to be me anymore, and that in itself is proof that God is real.

I want grace and love and redemption to be the core aspects of who I am. I want that to be what guides my choices and decisions, because without those things, we wouldn't even be here. That's Jesus, that's life, and I'm pretty pumped about it.

I told a friend at work yesterday that I was writing a memoir, and at first I don't think he believed me. Seeing that our only conversations have been about me dropping glasses and him finding my clumsiness hilarious, how once I put my waitress apron on I develop a severe case of short term memory loss, or bets on who can find the most cliche Southerner for the day, I don't really blame him. People get surprised when they find out I have a bit of a deep side to me and sometimes I like that. I like surprising people with my brain and my emotional depth. I like catching people off guard when they find out my only emotion isn't happiness. They all call me Sweet Little Jackie G and say that I could never hurt a fly. One time a coworker of mine looked at me and said, "Jackie, have you ever been through anything bad at all? You're just so happy all the time. Like seriously, what's the hardest thing you could have ever been through?" I hope he finds a copy of my book somewhere so that his question can have an answer.

It's getting to that point where I'm supposed to be thinking of all the deepest life lessons I've experienced and make them sound really pretty for a nice little ending to my story. I'm supposed to be spitting out future bumper sticker quotes and t-shirt logos right about now, but honestly all I want to do is tell you thank you. Thank you for reading my book. I seriously can't believe I did this, but mostly, I can't believe my mom was right. I mean come on, I was supposed to be a dinosaur hunter, not a writer.

I think my favorite part about writing this book for you is that it was pretty messy. I mean I've never written one before this so I'm not sure if this is the normal process, but working on this book has felt more like a journal entry than anything else. There were times when I was writing about things that happened years ago, and there were times when I was writing about things that are happening right now. That's where it got the most vulnerable. It's easy to write about lessons that I've learned in the past, even when those are hard lessons that involved me making some pretty bad mistakes. But honestly you guys, it's hard to think of anything that's more vulnerable than letting someone into something that doesn't have an answer. It's the times when I don't have the "moral of the story" ending that it just hurts to show. But hey, you know what? That's life. That's my biggest lesson I can think of to talk about right now. Letting people into the process, letting people see you when you do in fact look and feel like a hot mess is not exactly the easiest thing in the world to do. I get insecure when I don't have answers sometimes, but sitting in it alone still doesn't make sense to me. I know I'm only 22 and I'm saying things that make me sound like I've lived this big, long life, but I've hit a point in my story where I'm finding out what the most important thing in the world to have as a part of that, and the answer is people. Having people in not just the pretty parts where you're feeling extroverted and social and want to go ride Razor scooters, but having people in the places that aren't so pretty. Letting people see you in your unresolved problems, letting people know the parts of your story that you're ashamed of. Life doesn't make any sense without that, and that's becoming more and more clear every single day.

When I moved to Nashville, one of the things I was most excited for was to be in a new city where nobody knew me. I was so excited to be in a room full of people who didn't know my past, didn't know my story, and if I told them I was a professional foosball player, they wouldn't have any reason to not believe me. *"I can be whoever I want!"* I would think to myself. Little did I know that I could do that anywhere, and no matter what, I was going to just be myself in the long run anyway. I was so excited for the blank canvas this city represented to me. Then a month or so later I was visiting LA after one of the most traumatising experiences I've ever had.

The details are irrelevant, but just know that I was a complete wreck. That's when it hit me; nobody knew me. The thing I was the most excited for in this new city was now my biggest obstacle. If nobody knew me, then how was anyone truly going to be able to be there for me? In LA I had people that made me feel safe because they knew me. It was easy for me to cry in front of them, be my true self (which was a mess at the time), and everything because they knew me. That's what made it safe. I got on the plane back to Nashville and had never felt more alone in my life. I looked around me, strangers everywhere. I was going back to my new home in a city where, like I said before, if people heard I was a professional foosball player they'd believe me. Guys, I'm terrible at foosball.

You can bet your very last bottom dollar that the first thing I did when I got back to Tennessee was work on becoming known. I suddenly didn't want to be the mysterious new girl anymore, I wanted to find people to know my stuff. So I began to have the hard conversations, I began the risky investments into real friendship by sharing my story with people. Hiding was no longer an option. I needed people and I needed them fast.

Having people in your life that know every part of you is the best thing you can ever do for yourself. People who know your story but love you anyway, they're actually a very key part of life. When I started to experience the pain behind that not being in my life at the moment, I realized that it was actually an emergency. I realized that I didn't just want that, my soul needed that.

We were created to be known. That's what still blows my mind about Jesus, he knows us and loves us anyway. He sees us, mismatching socks and all and loves us anyway. But why?

If you've ever experienced grace before, not just the defini-
tion and knowledge of what grace means and what not, but actually
having a gut-wrenching wake up call experience with it, then you'll
understand how I felt in the moment when Alex responded to me
the day that I drove to her house to tell her what I had done.

Think about the worst thing you've ever done or could ever
think about doing, carrying it for years, then being completely forgiven and wiped clean of it for actually no logical reason at all. Think
about the one person who you're scared of finding out the naked
truth about who you are the most, then having them find out and
still love you anyway. Having them know you, broken shattered
pieces and all, and hugging you and loving you anyway. That's the
living definition of grace. That's the heart of Jesus.

Alex gifted me with that kind of grace that night. Minus the
fact that halfway through me telling her what happened she had to
put on her sneakers to run around the neighborhood in the middle
of the night out of how mad she was at Steve, all she could do was
remind me that she loved me and forgave me.

On January 5th, 2015 I was set free. I felt like I had been carrying around this shame story like a ball and chain, and suddenly
it was unlocked and the ball and chain wasn't a thing anymore. The
parts of me that I was so terrified of being found out were finally
gone. I could take the bandaid off the wounds and give them air to
heal. Now it didn't matter who knew that story about me because
I had the forgiveness and grace that had the power to heal me. It's
a feeling that I can't describe really, but for the first time I was able
to understand what it was like to feel the genuine power that grace
has to save the lives of the hopeless, broken humanity we're born

into. It was a type of grace that didn't have any ifs, ands, or buts to it. There were no ulterior motives, no paybacks, no nothing. Motivated purely by love, I was gifted with grace. Grace is our covering. It's how we survive.

The thing about grace is that in reality, I need it just as much as the next guy. I'm sorry if this comes across as offensive, but I need grace just as much as you, your mom, your mom's mom, everyone. We all need it, but do we all know it? Have we all come to terms with it? Jesus said, "Blessed are the poor in spirit, for theirs is the kingdom of Heaven." I've wrestled with that verse on more than one occasion, but as I sit here in this coffee shop, yet again disappointed at my empty cappuccino mug, I feel like this verse means exactly that. Some people can see how broken they are and some can't. But the awareness does not change the fact that they're equally broken. The only difference is that the ones who are aware about how poor in spirit they are are the ones who recognize their need for Jesus. They're the ones who hear who Jesus is and what he's done for them and run to him. If all this Jesus stuff is real, then after seeing their brokenness, the only thing that can possibly come next is grace. Not the textbook version, the real life version that can sting a little. The only way someone is able to experience that to its fullest depth is if they truly can see how much they need it. That's why facing my demons and accepting the truth behind my imperfections is the best thing I have ever done. Going on this journey of healing my heart, reflecting on my past and bringing it to the light for others to see is the greatest experience I've ever had. No, I'm not crazy enough to try to tell you that it's fun to have problems. I'm not saying that it's a joy to feel pain and make mistakes. Bawling my eyes out on my way to

Pasadena to tell my sister what I had done that night was not exactly the number one thing I would have chosen to do on like, my birthday or something. But I needed it, and coming to terms with that is what changed my life. Having the curtains lifted up to show my deepest flaws and regrets was the only way I would have ever been able to feel the life giving power grace has to offer. I wish I could pick a different word other than grace because it's just getting repetitive here, and according to my 7th grade english teacher repetitiveness is bad, but there's really no other way of putting it. If someone doesn't know they're broken, how would they ever feel the power of forgiveness? If someone can't accept their imperfections, how can they accept the grace that is meant to come along with it?

I've been wanting to get this tattoo that says "be free" from John 8 where Jesus says, "If the Son sets you free, you will be free indeed." I actually wanted to get that tattoo last year instead of "faith," but it didn't feel right yet because I didn't feel like it had its full purpose yet. This morning for the first time, I finally started to realize that I indeed am free. I'm free from my mistakes, free from my shame, free from my guilt, addictions, insecurities, fears, everything.

I was told a year and a half ago that I wasn't walking in freedom with Jesus. I was told that I would never be able to walk in freedom until I told my sister the truth about what had happened and about what I had done.

When I finally came clean to my sister and drove to her house in a puddle of snot and an obnoxiously loud crying mess, I thought that was it for me. I thought that her decision on to forgive me or not was what decided if I was truly forgiven. I thought that if she didn't forgive me, then I was forever unforgiven. I thought that was it for me, and that I would be defective and broken forever. But if she did forgive me, I would be saved and set free. If I had the forgiveness of my sister, everything would be okay.

This morning, I realized that I was wrong. Until this morning, I had been under the impression that my sister's choice to forgive me that day had the authority to decide who I was. In other words, I was making my sister my God. My sister is pretty cool and everything, but in no way on earth should she, or any human being ever have the kind of authority over someone's life like that. If I gave her forgiveness the power to truly release me, then what happens if she doesn't? What happens if we actually don't have a relationship afterwards? Or what if later down the road another conflict happens between us and that peace isn't there? Am I no longer forgiven?

As strange is it may sound, the truth of all this is that I never actually needed my sister's forgiveness to be free. I never needed her acceptance to be okay. Yes, I know that telling her was the right decision, but the harder I think about it the more I realize that I didn't even have to do that in order to be forgiven and free. I know I might sound crazy, but just bear with me here for a minute.

What if what Jesus said about us being forgiven for everything that we've done by simply believing in him was true? What if he actually meant it when he said he already took the shame and judgment for us on the cross? What if the grace God says he's given us that covers the worst thing we could have ever done is real? I think it is.

That right there is why I'm free. That right there is why I'm forgiven. My sister loving and forgiving me is a beautiful thing that I'm beyond thankful for, but it never had the power to tell me who I was. Only the grace of God has that power, and I had the grace of

God the whole time. It actually blows my mind thinking that I had the opportunity to walk in freedom all along. Shame never had the power to tell me who I was.

Our freedom already belongs to us. Our healing already belongs to us. We just have to take it. We have to reach out and, by faith, accept that it's already ours. Nobody can ever take that away from you or me, and that is one of the coolest parts about who Jesus is. He's untouchable.

I guess that tattoo has some meaning now. I should probably save up my money and go get it.

Now when someone tells me that they love me, I believe them. That's why knowing that God, the creator of the world, the all-perfect being who actually knows every mistake we've ever made and thought we've ever thought, loves us deeper than our little tiny human brains will ever be able to fully understand is a pretty big deal. He doesn't love some version of us we feel safe bringing to the table; he loves everything. He loves the cracks, the stains, all of it. That's a pretty big deal. This story shows that being known is worth it, but this story is proof that you are already free.

Acknowledgments

Thank you, Megan, Lauren, and Amy for being some of the greatest, most inspiring women I've ever met. Thank you for encouraging me so much on this journey, and for teaching me how to do friendship the way it was intended to be.

Thank you, Lizzie, for loving me so much when I needed it the most and for encouraging me to share my story. Your heart and life have inspired me in more ways than you'll ever know

Thank you, Sehler and Sydney, for never leaving my side through all the changes and transitions that life has taken us on. You two have no idea how much you mean to me.

Thank you, Eva, for creating such a safe home away from home for me to be. Thank you for reminding me what truly matters in life, and for listening to me talk about rollerblading and shirley temples all the time.

Thank you, Abbie, for always telling me the truth and teaching me how to be bold and believe in myself.

Thank you, Eppic, for being my friend, for watching out for me out in LA and for watching all the TV shows with me over our bowls of cereal.

Thank you, Alex, for never giving up on me, and continuing to have my back through our crazy story. Thank you for playing Pollies with me even when you didn't want to, and thank you for yelling at my friends for me in high school when they were mean to me. Oh, and for letting me wear all your clothes.

Thank you, Mom and Dad, for being willing to do literally anything for me. Mom, you apparently always knew I was going to be a writer, so thank you for encouraging me in that and staying up late with me studying vocab words in elementary school so I could get a good grade on my Word Power tests. Dad, thank you for giving me a sense of humor and for teaching me how to throw a baseball. I couldn't have done any of this without you two.

Thank you, Trinity, for editing my book. It means so much that you believed in me, and I am honored to have worked with you.

Thank you, Eva, for giving me a photo shoot in the 100 degree weather for my book promotion.

Thank you, Jordy, for building me a website and helping take care of me out here in Nashville.

Thank you Blake for playing catch with me and going on adventures on any and all hours of the day.

Thanks to Bartaco, for giving me some funny stories to tell and supplying me with a job through all of this.

Thank you, Donald Miller, for (obviously) being my favorite author and writing things that I could only dream I could write. Your words inspired me to write mine.

Thank you, Bob Goff, for picking up the phone one time when I called you and telling me to write a book.

Thank you to all my English teachers that taught me all the things. Mrs. Feller, shout out to you specifically.

Thank you to all the coffee shops I sat in: The Well, Three Brothers, Barista Parlor, Red Bicycle, Pinewood Social, Steadfast, Eighth and Roast, and all the rest that I can't remember. I spent quite a lot of money on coffee throughout the process of this book.

Thank you to my Patreon family. You all made it possible for me to be able to do what I love for a living. None of this would have been possible without you, so thank you for believing in me so much. Thank you to everyone who gave to help this book become a book.

I would never have been able to write this book without these people, so thank you from the bottom of my heart for this my friends.

And thank YOU for reading my book! You're giving this purpose. Now it's time for you to go write your own.

More Information

Join Jackie's online ministry and become a part of her family here:
www.patreon.com/jackiegtv

For information on Jackie Gronlund, please visit:

www.jackieg.tv

Become Jackie's internet friend by following her on social media:

@jackieg.tv

Watch Jackie's (sometimes embarrassing) YouTube videos here:

www.youtube.com/jackiegtv